THE WILD HEART OF FLORIDA

SELECTED AND EDITED BY JEFF RIPPLE AND SUSAN CERULEAN

UNIVERSITY PRESS OF FLORIDA

Gainesville Tallahassee Tampa Boca Raton Pensacola Orlando Miami Jacksonville

The Wild Heart of

FLORIDA

FLORIDA WRITERS ON FLORIDA'S WILDLANDS

Copyright 1999 by the Board of Regents of the State of Florida
Printed in the United States of America on acid-free recycled paper with soy ink
All rights reserved
Approximately $.85 of every book sold goes to the Florida chapter
of The Nature Conservancy.

04 03 02 01 00 99 6 5 4 3 2 1

LIBRARY OF CONGRESS CATALOGING-IN-PUBLICATION DATA
The wild heart of Florida: Florida writers on Florida's wildlands /
selected and edited by Jeff Ripple and Susan Cerulean.
p. cm.
ISBN 0-8130-1653-3 (cloth: alk. paper)—ISBN 0-8130-1656-8 (paper: alk. paper)
1. Natural history—Florida. 2. Nature conservation—Florida.
I. Ripple, Jeff, 1963- . II. Cerulean, Susan.
QH105.F6W48 1999
508.759—dc21 98-42184

The University Press of Florida is the scholarly publishing agency for the State
University System of Florida, comprised of Florida A & M University, Florida
Atlantic University, Florida International University, Florida State University,
University of Central Florida, University of Florida, University of North Florida,
University of South Florida, and University of West Florida.

University Press of Florida
15 Northwest 15th Street
Gainesville, FL 32611–2079
http://nersp.nerdc.ufl.edu/~upf

*With the deepest respect, we dedicate this book
to the memory of Marjorie Carr and to everyone
working to protect Florida's wild heart.*

Contents

Foreword

FOREVER WILD

*If I were to name the three most precious resources of life,
I should say books, friends, and nature; and the greatest
of these, at least the most constant and always at hand, is
nature. Nature we have always with us, an inexhaustible
storehouse of that which moves the heart, appeals to the
mind, and fires the imagination—health to the body,
a stimulus to the intellect, and joy to the soul.*
JOHN BURROUGHS

The smell of fresh salt air on deep-sea fishing trips and afternoons spent exploring hardwood hammocks remain fond childhood memories. When I was eight, my family moved to Marathon, the heart of the Florida Keys. I couldn't wait for summer break to spend my days snorkeling along the banks, chasing away barracudas and admiring the stingrays and starfish. Life prospered in this tropical paradise.

I grew up with a deep respect for Florida's natural heritage and a desire to preserve its majestic beauty. Each year, millions of visitors seek the experiences I took for granted as a child.

In the Keys, much has changed in the last twenty-five years. Now, driving down u.s. 1, my eyes are drawn to shell shops, motels, and gas stations. Development replaced the wildlands I once explored. The coral reefs are dying from overuse and pollution. I have to wonder what legacy we are leaving for our children. Will they have the opportunity to experience the natural beauty of the Florida Keys as I had? Aldo Leopold wrote, "Wilderness is a resource which can shrink but not grow . . . the creation of new wilderness in the full sense of the word is impossible."

Florida's fragile ecosystems continue to be lost at an alarming rate. Since 1936, many of our original natural communities have been converted to pavement, shopping centers, housing, and industrial uses. We have lost 40 percent of our original marshlands. Longleaf pine forests, once 51 percent of the state's pinelands, have declined from 7.6 million to fewer than one million acres. Nearly 80 percent of the ancient scrub communities of central Florida have been eliminated. We have lost 98 percent of the Miami rock ridge pinelands.

As we lose Florida's diverse landscapes, we lose the plants and animals that rely on these habitats for survival. Native Florida flora and fauna that have only recently become extinct include the dusky seaside sparrow, Caribbean monk seal, and the Rock Key devil's claws. State and federal agencies list 17 percent of Florida's wildlife as endangered, threatened, or of special concern. Among these rare creatures are the Florida panther, black bear, Key deer, and West Indian manatee, in addition to the American crocodile, which includes only Florida in the U.S. portion of its range.

The destruction of wildlands impacts humans as well. Our quality of life diminishes as natural areas are replaced with subdivisions and commercial sites. Communities become fragmented and ecosystems break down. Lakes and rivers are polluted by nutrients and sediment from agricultural and urban runoff. Critical recharge of aquifers becomes limited, reducing our groundwater supplies. Uncontrolled growth and development will eliminate the very essence of natural Florida.

But there is room for optimism. Floridians have long recognized the need to protect our remaining significant natural areas. Local communities across the state have voluntarily raised their taxes to purchase and manage environmentally sensitive lands. At the state level, several land acquisition programs have received funding for years.

In 1990, the Commission on the Future of Florida's Environment found that existing funding levels were insufficient to adequately protect our ecological systems, fish and wildlife habitat, biological diversity, upland forests, recreational lands, and open space. The Commission recommended a substantial increase to protect Florida's remaining natural lands before they were lost forever. That same year, Governor Bob Martinez and the Florida Legislature responded by enacting Preservation 2000, a ten-year, $3 billion land conservation program. Preservation 2000 funds go to purchase conservation and recreation lands, protect water resources, and acquire additions to our state parks, forests, and wildlife management areas. Preservation 2000 also helps local governments comply with growth management plans by providing grants for open space acquisition.

Today, Florida's many endangered ecosystems are being preserved with Preservation 2000 funds. Among the most noteworthy is the Everglades, the largest freshwater marsh in the United States. The Everglades, or the River of Grass as many call it, provides habitat for the endangered Florida panther, bald eagle, eastern indigo snake, and sandhill crane. Because it filters water from the Kissimmee River,

Lake Okeechobee, and the Everglades Agricultural Area, protection for the Everglades is critical to preserve Florida Bay—one of the nation's most productive marine estuaries—and the coral reefs in the Keys. A healthy system is crucial to ensure the future water supply for south Florida. Preservation 2000 funds are being used to acquire lands that will help restore the flow of fresh water to Florida Bay and protect lands buffering the East Everglades.

In central Florida, the ancient scrub of the Lake Wales Ridge is one of the most critically endangered ecosystems in the world. Scrub is Florida's most endemic natural community, with a biological diversity found nowhere else on earth; the central ridge alone harbors twenty-three federally endangered or threatened plants. Thanks to public acquisition of scrub through Preservation 2000, plants and animals will continue to exist on the Lake Wales Ridge as they have for 25 million years.

Apalachicola Bay's estuarine system is among the most productive in the northern hemisphere, supporting a strong commercial and sport fishing industry. The bay produces 90 percent of all oysters consumed in our state and 10 percent of all oysters consumed nationwide. The surrounding wilderness shelters the endangered Florida black bear and at least eighteen endangered plant species. Preservation 2000 funds helped acquire Tate's Hell, a vast swamp that borders the Apalachicola National Forest and drains into Apalachicola Bay. This buffer will safeguard the bay and its bounty forever.

Our most famous river, the Suwannee, hosts Florida's largest whitewater rapids, the state's largest waterfall, and an underwater cave system. Florida manatees, Gulf sturgeons, and alligator snapping turtles are among the endangered species that find shelter in the river and its many springs. In addition to protecting land along the river, Preservation 2000 funds have preserved famous freshwater springs and pristine hardwood swamps throughout the area.

Some of the world's most beautiful beaches stretch along the Panhandle coast. The Topsail Hill property contains some of the tallest sugar-sand dunes in the state, with a system of freshwater lakes nestled behind the dunes. Florida's east coast beaches and coastal scrublands provide habitat for many rare species, including loggerhead and green sea turtles, scrub jays, and gopher tortoises. Through Preservation 2000, these unique coastal ecosystems are being preserved.

There is no doubt that we have made great strides in protecting our natural areas with programs like Preservation 2000. Acquisition is simply the first step in the long-term preservation of our wildlands. Without proper stewardship, these lands will lose their natural resource value. A commitment to resource-based management is essential for maintaining the natural character of our ecosystems.

Land managers face many challenges in addressing the effects of past, present, and future human activities on our wildlands. In the past, Florida's natural areas maintained their health through naturally occurring lightning fires. Today, development has fragmented our natural areas into smaller pockets, making it impossible for wildfires to effectively sweep across the land. Prescribed fires must now be used to imitate the historic natural force and decrease the threat of destructive fires.

Exotic species control and removal is a critical component of land management. In south Florida alone, more than 400 species of exotic (introduced) plants are invading our natural lands. Left unchecked, species including melaleuca, Australian pine, and Brazilian pepper will completely overtake or destroy native vegetation, forever altering the landscape. Efforts are underway to eradicate these species, but more must be done.

Our wildlands must also be managed for the enjoyment and benefit of residents and visitors. This has been a clear goal of Florida's land acquisition programs. Our lakes, rivers, forests, bays, and beaches provide numerous opportunities to recreate in some of Florida's finest natural areas. These places bring us closer to nature and instill a deeper appreciation for natural Florida.

Florida has been the nation's leader in public land acquisition. However, our job is far from complete. Even under public ownership, wildlands remain threatened. There have been recent attempts to surplus conservation lands for other purposes including prisons and town centers. These facilities are needed, but not at the expense of our natural areas. We must continue to support state and local policies that keep land and water conservation a top priority. Funding for acquisition and management of conservation lands must continue the green infrastructure created through Preservation 2000.

Many of our imperiled ecosystems remain vulnerable to development. While public ownership is crucial, we also need to work with landowners to provide incentives for protecting wildlife habitat on private lands. Additional funds will be necessary to guarantee the long-term resource management of our wildlands.

Each year, 325,000 new residents move to Florida. They are attracted by Florida's natural beauty. As our population continues to grow, we will be faced with tough choices. Growth and a healthy economy must go hand in hand with the preservation of our wildlands. Local land-use decisions will become increasingly important as we seek to balance the needs of our increasing population while also maintaining the quality of life that makes Florida an attractive place to live and work.

Over the last six years, I had the opportunity to work at both the state and local levels to protect Florida's conservation lands. I was inspired by the many citizens committed to protecting their natural heritage. Grassroots efforts across the state succeeded in raising millions of dollars to purchase environmentally sensitive lands through local bond referendums. Broad local support has been critical to the ongoing funding of our state programs including Preservation 2000. We must continue to inform policy makers about the need to protect our wildlands. Florida's future will be brighter because of our efforts. I have hope that with continued vigilance, future generations will experience natural Florida as we know it today.

Debbie Drake
Former Director of Government Relations
The Nature Conservancy

Preface

The Wild Heart of Florida: Florida Writers on Florida's Wildlands is a compilation of nineteen creative essays by some of the state's most talented writers celebrating the natural heritage of Florida. The essays are stories of what Floridians have lost and found and could still lose again. The authors are all Floridians, though many are not native and some have now left to lead their lives in other states. As novelists, journalists, poets, and artists, we celebrate and give thanks for what has been conserved in Florida. But there remain another 2.3 million acres, considered by biologists to be environmentally significant and irreplaceable, that are still in need of protection. Like many rare and beautiful things, the Florida landscape is at risk. Our state's native ecosystems, including longleaf pine, coral reef, coastal beach, and scrub, have been deemed the most endangered among the fifty states. We have drained more than half of our wetlands and developed most of our upland scrub and sandhills to accommodate enormous population growth, plundering a great wealth of plants and animals and transforming water into a precious commodity in many urban and agricultural areas.

To the credit of all Floridians, the state had the foresight to create Preservation 2000 (P–2000), considered the nation's leading land acquisition program, a model that other states emulate. The ten-year program began in 1990 and has made possible the purchase of nearly 900,000 acres of environmentally critical land. Lands purchased and protected include beaches in the Archie Carr National Wildlife Refuge (considered among the most important nesting sites for loggerhead sea turtles in the world), threatened scrub in central Florida, the sandy dunes of Topsail Hill in the Panhandle, and North Key Largo Hammock in the Florida Keys. Another 800,000 acres could be acquired before the program ends in the year 2000. P–2000 has been a good first effort. Floridians have reason to be proud of their accomplishment. But P–2000 must not be the final word for land conservation in Florida.

There is a silent majority of citizens who believe that natural areas and the varied lifeforms they support must be preserved. But—with the exception of small bands of overworked conservation advocates—who speaks for Florida's beleaguered landscape and the programs intended to protect it? In the western United States, a solid contingent of artists and writers elevate both the plight and the beauty of nature in the public eye so that all may understand and delight in the connections between art and nature. Here in Florida, where native status can be claimed by few and is generally undervalued, the artists and writers who speak for our wild places are not so well known. But we have been taking note and are speaking amongst ourselves and in public forums, as all of us must, on behalf of this fragile landscape we love and call home.

The Wild Heart of Florida is the first collection of contemporary nature writing about Florida. Most of the authors describe wild places that are special to them, some weave their thoughts about Florida's disappearing native environment with their concerns about what will be left for their children, some follow the struggle to have sensitive wildlands protected, many look back to what we have lost and forward to what we might yet save, and others speak with hope of reestablishing the old oral and written tradition of story we seem to have forsaken with our connection to the land.

All of the authors have donated their time and talent to contribute to *The Wild Heart of Florida*. The royalties for the book are being donated to The Nature Conservancy–Florida Chapter to help them continue their conservation work in the state. A copy of *The Wild Heart of Florida* will be given at no charge to every state legislator, the governor and his cabinet, and U.S. representatives and senators from Florida as a statement of our commitment to preserving Florida's natural heritage.

The Wild Heart of Florida is a creative work, not a scientific text, though the facts underpinning the essays are true. Some of these stories may evoke a sense of loss or love or outrage, and that is our intention. We want you to think hard about the mark you will make on the land. We offer you these words as our contribution toward "restorying" the human inhabitants of Florida. It is time to break the silence. The future of Florida's wildlands depends on this.

Jeff Ripple
Susan Cerulean
May 1998

Acknowledgments

We would first like to thank the authors for the generous donation of their work; Ken Scott of the University Press of Florida for his support and advice regarding this project; the Carr family for permission to reprint Archie Carr's "The Bird and the Behemoth"; and the Florida chapter of The Nature Conservancy, particularly the Lake Wales Ridge and Tallahassee offices, for their enthusiastic assistance. We would be remiss if we did not acknowledge Stephen Trimble and Terry Tempest Williams for their compilation *Testimony: Writers of the West Speak on Behalf of Utah Wilderness*, which inspired the present form of *The Wild Heart of Florida* and provided an example that we could follow to convey our gratitude for the accomplishments of the Preservation 2000 program and our concern about the future of Florida's wildlands to government and the public.

We also thank the following rightsholders for permission to publish or reprint the selections in this book:

Bill Belleville, "A Valley of Inches: The Headwaters of the Upper St. Johns River," excerpted from *The St. Johns: The Unseen River*, a work in progress. Copyright 1997 by Bill Belleville. Published with permission of the author.

Al Burt, "A Life in the Scrub," first publication. Copyright 1997 by Al Burt. Published with permission of the author.

Archie Carr, "The Bird and the Behemoth," from *Ulendo: Travels of a Naturalist In and Out of Africa*. Copyright 1964 by Alfred A. Knopf Publishers. Reprinted with permission of the publisher and the author's family.

Susan Cerulean, "'Restorying' Florida." Copyright 1997 by Susan Cerulean. Published with permission of the author.

Susan Cerulean, "The Wild Heart of Florida," from a work in progress. Copyright 1997 by Susan Cerulean. Published with permission of the author.

Lola Haskins, "A Florida Marriage," adapted from her foreword for *Visions of Florida* (by Woody Walters), University Press of Florida, 1993. Copyright 1997 by Lola Haskins. Published with permission of the author.

Julie Hauserman, "The Ugliest Beach in Florida," first publication. Copyright 1997 by Julie Hauserman. Published with permission of the author.

Carl Hiaasen, "Last of the Falling Tide," from *Heart of the Land*, published by The Nature Conservancy, 1994. Copyright 1994 by Carl Hiaasen. Reprinted with permission of the author.

Joe Hutto, "River of Dreams," first publication. Copyright 1997 by Joe Hutto. Published with permission of the author.

Jeff Klinkenberg, "Brooker Creek," from the *St. Petersburg Times*.

About The Nature Conservancy

The Nature Conservancy is an international, nonprofit, membership organization. Its mission is to preserve plants, animals, and natural communities that represent the diversity of life on Earth by protecting the lands and waters they need to survive. Since 1950, The Nature Conservancy has protected more than ten million acres in fifty states and Canada. It has also helped partner organizations preserve millions of acres in Latin America and the Caribbean. The Conservancy owns and manages more than 1,500 preserves—the largest private system of nature sanctuaries in the world.

The Nature Conservancy saves critical natural areas by setting them aside through purchase, gift, or conservation easement. The Conservancy works in partnership with many private organizations, as well as local, state, and federal agencies, to facilitate land purchases, build public support for conservation, and manage land.

The Florida chapter of The Nature Conservancy is comprised of some 45,000 individuals, foundations, and corporations who have helped protect more than 700,000 acres of Florida's natural lands and waters since 1959. Currently, the Conservancy oversees the care of more than 36,300 natural acres in Florida. The Conservancy also helps design and implement methods for managing thousands of acres of publicly owned land.

The Nature Conservancy maintains offices in key centers of Florida's most imperiled areas, including the Apalachicola Basin, Florida Keys, Indian River Lagoon, Kissimmee Valley, and Lake Wales Ridge. To learn more about the Florida chapter, contact:

The Nature Conservancy, Florida Chapter
222 South Westmonte Drive, #300
Altamonte Springs, FL 32714
(407) 682-3664
(407) 682-3077

THE WILD HEART OF FLORIDA

"Restorying" Florida

SUSAN CERULEAN

Without stories, we do not know who we are,
nor what we might become.
D. H. LAWRENCE

The word "restoration" implies refilling, curing, setting right, caring for what has been injured. There are many hopeful examples of such landscape healings throughout Florida at present, from the Keys to the Ocklawaha River, from Tate's Hell Swamp to the Everglades. But it seems to me that even more will be required, beyond the considerable challenges of eliminating exotic plants, restoring natural flooding, and bringing back summer fire, if we are to truly heal all that ails our state.

That which we have overlooked is a "restorying" of the human inhabitants of Florida. Our population of 14 million is remarkably transient and overwhelmingly unfamiliar with our landscapes. Al Burt has written eloquently about the "absentee hearts" of many

Floridians, whose bodies and winter homes are currently lodged in our state, but whose loyalties, and hearts, reside elsewhere.

It has not always been so.

The first humans arrived in Florida toward the end of the Pleistocene epoch, about 12,000 years ago, when much of North America was still covered with glaciers. Enormously complex and resilient native societies lived on this peninsula, fishing, collecting shellfish, hunting, gathering wild plants, and sometimes cultivating crops. Innumerable middens and mounds offer silent testimony to the Calusa, the Apalachee, the Tequesta, the Timucuan, the Hobe, the Matecumbe, the Tobago, and many others. They were threaded into their landscape like the palm fiber they wove into rope, and they knew well the plants and animals with whom they shared space, and had a name for each, and a story.

The root of our inability to imagine and create a hopeful, inclusive vision for Florida probably lies in the waves of European conquistadors who invaded Florida between 1500 and 1800 A.D., exterminating or driving out all our native inhabitants. With the genocide of the original peoples, we lost a profound opportunity to understand our landscape.

Why are the old stories that sprang from intimate contact with land so important to our present ecological dilemmas? Embedded in them is an old, old knowledge of how animals, including the human animal, can interact and cooperate with one another in a sustainable fashion. A shared oral or written tradition explains to us the land and its creatures and how they all relate. This context may be what keeps people home, tending the land and their lives within it.

However, in Florida, such a body of knowledge, accrued through 14,000 years of living in harmony on the land, has been superseded by 400 years of raid and pillage, greed, and an unengaged sort of tourism. These relatively new relationships to Florida are still the dominant paradigm today. The motives for coming to Florida, for most, have not included an interest in the fullness of what we are here. Florida State University religion professor Leo Sandon speaks of the two primary opportunities with which Florida has been identified through the years: a legitimized opportunity to raid and pillage, and an invitation to experience a tropical Eden.

The problem with both visions of Florida is that they do little to establish a sense of Florida as home. The first focuses on our ownership and development of the state, rather than on identification or kinship with it. The second dreams of this land as an enchanting but temporary place, a diversion from real life, a location where we might enjoy either our vacation or our retirement.

What does it mean to live on unstoried land? How does such poverty of heritage relate to attachment and stewardship of a landscape? Without a story, without specifying the sacred, we can hold nothing holy, or whole. We desecrate, we drain, ditch and dike, because "we know not what we do." Nor where we really are, nor what makes this place work.

What we need in Florida today, in theologian John Cobb's words, are new stories that "serve wellness, that move us towards a new narrative of restoration and hope, that recognize terrestrial intelligence."

I have a strong hunch that the real stories of Florida are so powerful, so gripping, so various, and so enriching that if we were to somehow reclaim them and weave them into our culture, things would be very different in our state. The notion of security as we view it now would seem gray and dull, compared to the life in the living forests and springs and prairies.

Despite our impoverished cultural legacy, there is a clearly marked signpost back to our true heritage in this landscape. The landscape itself, despite its tragic losses, remains storied, reminds the Chickasaw poet Linda Hogan. Florida's many restoration projects and its conserved wild places offer physical and spiritual maps to us. Here is how to read them.

Lie with your ear to the ground. Let birdsong trace its complexities onto your eardrum. Walk with your face in the wind, and dive into the cold waters. Listen with your heart.

Tell that story.

FROM **A Land Remembered**

PATRICK D. SMITH

LAKE OKEECHOBEE AREA—1875

In 1875, Tobias MacIvey wanted to give a small herd of cattle to his Seminole friend Keith Tiger, who had a camp somewhere in the Big Cypress Swamp, the northern approach to the Everglades. In Punta Rassa he was instructed to follow the south bank of the Caloosahatchee River until it met a great lake called Okeechobee, go to the south shore, and then turn directly south until he found the swamp. The following excerpt from the novel A Land Remembered *paints a vivid picture of the Lake Okeechobee area as it once was.*

~ ~ ~

On the fourth day they struck the western shore of Okeechobee, marveling at the seemingly endless expanse of water before them. The shimmering surface stretched into the horizon and gave no hint of a distant shore. Vast areas of blooming pickerel weed lined the water's edge, creating a sea of soft blue that merged gently with clumps of willows and little islands of buttonbush with its creamy white flowers. Nearby rookeries exploded with birds, great blue herons and snowy egrets, white herons and wood ibises, whooping cranes and anhingas with their wings spread outward to dry them. Cormorants dove beneath the surface and popped up unexpectedly fifty feet away, startling flocks of ducks and coots that peppered the surface. Majestic roseate spoonbills stalked up and down the shallows, swishing their long paddle bills from side to side as they raked the bottom in search of food, their pink feathers catching the sunlight and making them appear even pinker.

Zech insisted they stop for a day or two and let the cattle graze on the abundant grass, but he was more interested in rest for his father than food for the cows. Tobias agreed reluctantly, wanting to push on immediately, but in his weakened condition he allowed himself to be overruled.

After making camp beneath a thick covering of alders, they walked back to the shore and watched the unfamiliar sights with fascination, seeing an endless parade of nature's creatures. Willows were so loaded with chattering red-winged blackbirds that it seemed the tree limbs would surely break, and fish were so plentiful their fins cut the calm surface with constant ripples.

Zech took his fishing line from the saddlebag, cut a cane pole, and caught crickets for bait; and in only moments he caught more black bass and catfish than they could hope to eat. On the way back to the camp he gathered figs from a thick grove of wild trees, and for supper they had fish roasted over an open fire, followed by the sugary fruit.

That night the eerie call of limpkins blended with the croaking of bullfrogs and the grunting of alligators, forming a strange type of music never heard out on the prairie. Tobias moved closer to the warming fire and said, "I'm glad we stopped here, Zech. I've never seen a place so full of life. Not even back in the scrub. I can see now why some of the Indians they ran off from here hid in the swamps, hoping to come back someday. I hope they can, but I got a notion they won't. When folks find out what's here they'll take it over, and you won't ever again see an Indian on this lake's shore. Maybe someday we can come back and see it all."

"I sure hope so. James Tiger told me there can be waves out there taller than a man, and at some places there's sand dunes like at the ocean. He also told me that the sun sucks water from the lake, and it'll drop down several inches during the day, and then during the night it'll come right back to where it was. I'd sure like to see that too."

"Maybe someday," Tobias said again. "But right now I think I'll sleep. I feel kinda tired all through and through, like a wore-out old ox."

"You ain't old at all, Pappa. But you get some rest. I'll stay up tonight and take care of the cows."

Two days stretched into three, and Tobias gained strength from the fresh fish, wild fruits and berries. On the morning of the third day they broke camp and continued the drive, skirting the rim of the lake, but when they rounded the western shore and attempted to head directly south, they were met by a stretch of sawgrass with blades so sharp it prohibited the entrance of cows, men and horses.

At this point they turned to the southwest and entered a custard-apple forest, a jungle unlike anything they had ever encountered. Trees were so dense they formed a barrier almost as impenetrable as the sawgrass. The sky was blocked out immediately by leafy branches completely covered by a solid blanket of moon vines, turning a bright noonday sun to dim twilight.

The cows walked single file to make their way through the wall of trunks, and there was no way to drive them in a straight line. They skirted masses of dead limbs long since blown down by hurricanes, and gourd vines looping from branch to branch formed a curtain of green fruit. Trees were peppered with air plants that blossomed with brilliant red and orange flowers, and the ground beneath was totally bare except for lush beds of ferns, some ground level and others as tall as the horses.

The forest also teemed with Carolina parakeets as numerous as were the blackbirds at the lake, and low-hanging limbs were anchored to the ground by giant spider webs. Once Zech threw a stick into one of the webs in a useless attempt to break through; it sang like violin strings and held fast, causing the huge brown and yellow spiders to rush forward and examine the captured missile.

Every foot of the way was blocked by something: trunks, tangling vines, webs, grotesque outcroppings of roots. They turned, zigzagged and backtracked, popping the whips and cursing the bewildered cows, moving tortuously through an atmosphere so murky they couldn't determine if they were heading south or north; and in one four-hour stretch they traveled less than a mile.

There was no sunset that afternoon beneath the solid roof of the jungle, only a fleeting moment when twilight turned to instant darkness. Zech built a fire and they huddled together, hearing the chilling cry of the sentinel hawks and the mournful song of whippoorwills. Screech owls then joined the chorus, making the cows come together in a tight circle. Zech suggested time and again they turn back and seek another way, but each time Tobias shook his head in disagreement.

It was impossible to tell when dawn came, and when finally a dim yellow light drifted down through the vines, it could as well have been noon as mid-morning. They moved again, repeating the experience of the previous day, turning, twisting and probing, mile after mile of the same frustration. Even Tobias now worried about the cows and horses since there was nothing for them to eat but ferns. He hoped the lacy outgrowths were not poisonous.

Another night was spent beneath the canopy, then another morning vainly searching for an escape route. Just when they both became resigned to the fact they were hopelessly trapped, they broke free at mid-afternoon and entered a marsh. The cows and horses grazed ravenously, and Tobias agreed to stop for the night.

After building a fire Zech walked back to the edge of the forest. He stepped gingerly onto the moon vines and jumped up and down, finding the green carpet to be as solid as a bed. Then he walked upward slowly, a step at a time, until he reached the top of the trees and stood on the jungle's roof.

The vines stretched away as far as he could see, like a verdant plain splotched with blooming white flowers. He walked forward, at first cautiously and then with confidence, traveling a hundred yards before turning back reluctantly, wishing he could retrace the entire distance they had come but knowing he should return to Tobias.

As he made his way down the leafy incline and onto solid ground again, he trembled with excitement, feeling he now had a newfound secret not to be shared, like a baby eagle no longer earthbound, drunk with the exhilaration of its first flight.

The thrill of the experience carried over past supper and into the night, and as they moved away at dawn, Zech looked back with both fear and joy at the giant tent nature had created over the forest.

The Curse of the Medallion

RANDY WAYNE WHITE

There was a lightning storm a few nights ago that knocked out the power on Pine Island where I live. You have to know the circumstances to understand why it brought to mind a lost civilization, a ceremonial gold medallion, the teenage boy who found it and who later died by his own hand.

I was a couple of miles offshore at the time, heading back from Cabbage Key in my Hewes flats skiff when—zap!—all lights vanished. The abruptness of it was disorienting. Those of us who live in solitary places think we know darkness. What we know is a diaphanous gray. When that grayness is unexpectedly extinguished, it is a little like stumbling toward the lip of an abyss.

I backed the throttle, killed the engine and waited. The rain hadn't reached me yet but there was wind. A Halloween moon gauged the altitude of cumulus towers. Much of Florida's west coast is fendered from the Gulf of Mexico by mangrove islands. Lightning blasts were a white strobe which illuminated a world that, like darkness, I thought I knew. Wrong again. Mangrove leaves were blue—not green. In the distance was boiling smoke—not rain. The village of Pineland on Pine Island was not a place of tin-roofed houses built on Indian shell mounds. It was a black thing elevated—a dinosaur shape afloat. It might have been the current year. It might have been a thousand years before. Cut the electrical umbilical and the eyes are quick to readjust to primal light.

I stood at the boat's wheel, feeling the wind, and I thought: This is the way it was when the Calusa were here. . . .

At the time of the Spanish contact in the sixteenth century, the Calusa's was a sophisticated society of fisher people, hunters and gatherers that dominated Florida's west coast. They and their predecessors built and lived on elaborate shell pyramids long before the time of Christ and two hundred years past the arrival of the Spaniards. In terms of achievement, the Calusa mounds are the South's equivalent of the Maya's Tikal, the Inca's Machupichu. In terms of human chronology, the high-rise hotels of Sarasota and the condominiums of Sanibel and Captiva islands are a few pale seconds in a long calendar day.

I am not a fanciful person. My house is built atop an Indian mound. I've never seen Calusa ghosts. I have never communicated with the spirits of people who lived and worshiped, reproduced and died on the hillsides I now use a Sarlo grass eater to mow. But when the island went black, the squall light created a curious tabular vacuum in which I could imagine the way it had been: black islands and the kind of spatial isolation that breeds demons . . . temple mounds that faced the setting sun . . . broad patios and ceremonial plazas . . . holding ponds for fish . . . canals dredged by hand that bisected islands and led to the sea . . . chikees and thatched-roofed long houses big enough to hold two thousand tribespeople . . . priests wearing wooden god-masks while presiding over human sacrifices ... artisans at work, weaving, carving, molding, painting ... mothers tending to royal heirs and the sons of kings who, according to early Spanish missionaries, wore a gold ornament on their foreheads as an insignia of rank ...

That's why I thought about the gold medallion when lightning knocked the power out. That's why I thought of the teenage boy who found it and who later died by his own hand.

~ ~ ~

As I told Dr. William Marquardt, curator in archaeology, Florida Museum of Natural History, "Considering all that happened before, all that's gone on since, you have to agree that parts of it sound like a Stephen King story."

Like most archaeologists, Marquardt is a pragmatist by training and a diplomat through necessity. "I'm willing to agree," he said, "that what happened was tragic. What has happened since is certainly alarming."

His tone was unequivocal—the events were alarming in terms of archaeology, had nothing to do with ghosts or the supernatural, or as some said, the curse of a long-gone tribe that was decimated by European diseases and then vanished.

We were off the coast in my skiff making a visual tour of the Calusa mounds. This was weeks after the squall zapped the power. The west coast of Florida was once again tropic-bright, vacation-friendly.

"The remarkable thing about the Calusa," Marquardt told me, "is that there's no uncontested evidence of horticulture, yet they managed a culturally complex society. They built permanent towns. They dug canals and built temple mounds. They developed elaborate art, a sophisticated religion and a political system that included tribute sent by chiefs under Calusa control—all dependent on highly pro-

ductive fishing methods. Unfortunately for us, that tribute sometimes included a tiny bit of gold and silver probably taken from
Spanish shipwrecks."

Unfortunate for archaeologists. Unfortunate for anyone interested in the pre-European history of the Americas.

"Of the sixty or so metal Calusa ornaments that have been
found," he added, "only four or five are gold. That's why it caused
such a fervor among amateurs when the boy found the medallion.
Sadly, most of the mounds show signs of that fervor."

This was our second day in the boat, yet we had visited only a few
of the major habitation sites that range from Charlotte Harbor to
Naples and beyond into Everglades National Park. Access to the island is not easy. To tourists charmed by Disney World and Florida's
other roadside attractions, the sites would be indistinguishable and
unappealing: a hedge of dense mangroves with an elevated nucleus
of gumbo limbo trees. Nearly all were reachable only by shallow-
draft skiff.

At each site, Marquardt and I would bushwhack our way through
monkey-bar prop roots, then into the island's interior. There were
sand flies and mosquitoes. There were vines and bayonet plants and
prickly pear cacti. The flora of Florida soon strangles anything that
does not move. Leave a plot of ground untended for a year and it will
become jungle. Most of these islands had been abandoned a century
or more ago by pioneer fishermen and farmers.

At one point—I was picking something out of my hand, a cactus
needle, maybe—I said to Marquardt, "You really enjoy busting your
butt to get to these places?"

Marquardt, who looks like one might expect a scientist to look—
eyeglasses, backpacker clothing, and sparse beard—is a precise and
methodical man. He is a gourmet cook and a musician. His interests
are far-flung, but his professional focus is laser-like: he's hell-bent
on protecting these mounds and funding a research center to study

the Calusa. "Sure," he said, "it's a lot better than being in the office." Then he waved at the haze of gnats orbiting his face. "But I could do without these damn bugs. People are still arguing about how the Indians endured them."

How the Calusa endured is puzzling enough, but how they managed to thrive is mind-boggling. Hack your way to a major site and it is a stunning thing to come upon high hills faced with football-sized whelk shells. In the mangrove littoral of west Florida, a 38-foot-high mound is the equivalent of Maroon Peak in Colorado—yet the mound is not supposed to be there. It, like others near it, was built by hand: constructed by workers—and, perhaps, slaves—who piled the shells and shaped the contours, basketfull after woven basketfull. Like modern-day developers who came later, these people piled their homes upon a swamp.

"That's why it's so damn sad what has happened to the mounds," Marquardt said. He was talking about the early and mid-1900s when road builders used them as fill. And he was talking about mounds that had been destroyed by dredging and by developers, and by the tenet of Florida's carrion-feeder economic ethic: The old girl's dying anyway, so go ahead and bite off a chunk.

But Marquardt was talking about the medallion, too.

At each site, cut deep into each mound, were a multitude of holes, some the size of bomb craters. Inside each, the ancient whelk and conch shells were bleached white. When stepped upon, they had the resonance of bones.

"Treasure hunters," Marquardt said. "Archaeologists all over the world have to contend with it. The thing is"—Marquardt had to smile in frustration when he said this—"there's nothing for them to find unless they're looking for old shells. Nothing they could sell! The Calusa were pot-breakers. It's unusual to find even a large pottery shard. They didn't have stone and the little bit of metal they had came from the Spaniards."

So what were they looking for?

"Something they'll never find in these mounds," Marquardt said. "They're looking for treasure buried by a pirate named José Gaspar. And they're looking for ceremonial ornaments, something like the boy found near here."

Marquardt was talking about a pirate who never existed. He was talking about a gold Calusa medallion that does.

~ ~ ~

In 1969, on an island off Florida's west coast, fourteen-year-old Rommie David Taylor and his younger brother were sifting for Indian artifacts when they began to find bones, a few Spanish chevron beads, and then a small, oddly designed pendant made of sheet gold. It was 64 mm long and 33 mm wide and weighed less than an ounce. Into the face of the medallion were etched concentric circles upon a cross, three bisecting lines, a pair of teardrop shapes, and nested half rectangles—like doors within doors—on the spatulated half. On the back were new-moon shapes, one above the other.

Some would say that the medallion resembled an alligator's head. Others would describe the etching as a "spider" design. According to Marquardt, "Some of these symbols go back to 200 B.C., but the short answer is that we don't really know what they mean."

Years later, the boy's mother, Lorraine, would tell me: "David was far more interested in archaeology than, say, baseball. He read everything he could about the history of the Calusa, and he liked to hunt for artifacts. It was uncanny the way he could find things. Like the medallion—he was digging in a place no one would think to look."

It is still not known for certain where the boy was digging, but it is likely that he had stumbled upon an interment field. He found the medallion among the rib bones of an intrusive burial—a fact that troubled the boy, according to his mother.

"He seemed to grow increasingly nervous as the weeks passed," she said. "He'd always been a good student but he had trouble concentrating on his homework. I know that he was having nightmares and he seemed to become obsessed with thoughts of Indians. It bothered him that he'd dug up a grave."

Lorraine also had nightmares. In one, she and her son were standing in water that was neck-deep. The boy had the medallion in his hand. He dropped it. In the dream, the mother begged him not to go after it, but he laughed and disappeared beneath the water.

Three days later, the boy hung himself from a very low tree—perhaps a fatal attempt to "experience unconsciousness," one Sheriff's Department investigator said. The medical examiner decided it was "death by misadventure."

It is a tragic story that gets worse. Lorraine was "nearly out of her mind" with grief, one family member said, when she was contacted by a local amateur treasure hunter. The treasure hunter told Lorraine that, if she was willing to attend a séance at his house, it might be possible for her to communicate with her dead son. At the séance, she, the treasure hunter and several others sat looking at a candle as David "spoke" through a series of raps on the table. The boy was asked if his mother should give the medallion to the treasure hunter. Two raps—yes. Lorraine did as she was told.

But life did not go smoothly for the treasure hunter once he had the artifact. When people found out what he had done, local reaction was so strong that he decided to move out of the area. Later, he would sell it, saying, "I'm glad to get rid of the damn thing."

The current owner—who lives within a few hundred yards of where the medallion was found and who prefers not to be identified—says that he's had his problems with the medallion, too. "A friend and I bought it just to get it away from the guy who cheated David's mother," he said. "We gave it to a third friend, no strings attached, with the stipulation that it be placed in a museum with

David's name on it. That never happened. Our friend was worried—correctly—that it would promote more looting. Even so, we began to bicker. One friend purchased the other friend's share. We bickered some more. It came so close to ruining our friendship that we began to joke about it—the curse of the medallion."

"I'm not superstitious," the owner added, "but it's absolutely true that I've given the thing away three times and each time it's ended up back in my hands. My Indian friends—who are superstitious—say that's because the medallion is meant to remain here."

I saw the medallion not long ago. I stood on a mound at sunset and held it. This was a couple of weeks after the island went black, after I'd seen the way it was when the Calusa dominated. Whether one is superstitious or not, it is a powerful thing to hold such an artifact while standing in the precise place where the kings who may have worn it once walked.

The medallion seemed too small to contain the weight of its own history. That I did not understand the etchings added to their gravity. The medallion glowed as if it had absorbed a thousand years of golden light, but its design seemed to imply the kind of darkness where islands assume the shapes of dinosaurs and where demons are feared.

"My Indian friends tell me I should rebury the thing," the owner said. "It may be the right thing to do."

~   ~   ~

"Discussing a find as rare as David Taylor's," Marquardt told me, "is a double-edged sword. When we publicize information about archaeological artifacts, we risk more damage to the mounds. On the other hand, the more people we educate about how much can be learned from the sites, the better chance we have that people will want to protect them. A Neighborhood Watch approach—we'd like to promote that."

We were now twenty-five miles from Fort Myers, roaming around the bayside village of Pineland on Pine Island, which is connected by a drawbridge to the mainland. Pineland is among the Florida Museum of Natural History's most important and ambitious projects. In 1895, Pineland—then known as Batty's Landing—was first described by Smithsonian ethnologist Frank Hamilton Cushing: "The foundations, graded ways, and canals here were greater . . . than any I had yet seen. The inner or central courts were enormous."

Amazingly, the Pineland site hasn't changed much since the days of Cushing. Its mounds were first protected by Prohibition-era houses built atop them, and then by two modern visionaries, Col. Donald and Patricia Randell, who bought up and preserved the mounds and donated the site to the University of Florida. These days, Marquardt and his team are working umpteen hours a week to solicit funding and to design the Randell Research Center, a permanent multidisciplinary outdoor lab and educational facility.

"A few years ago," Marquardt said, "three men were arrested for using a bulldozer—a bulldozer—on one of the remote islands. Using it to dig up the mounds. They completely destroyed one of the area's most important sites. You know why? They said they were looking for José Gaspar's treasure. It would be laughable if it wasn't so tragic."

Laughable because José Gaspar was the invention of a railroad company flack who, in 1919, needed a way to romanticize the mosquito-infested area, so he created Gaspar and his "captive women" to promote tourism and land sales on the "pirate coast." Later, Gaspar "historians" published booklets that contain "authentic" pirate maps where X marks the spot—and the spot is always an Indian. The fiction has been so widely accepted that Tampa has an annual José Gaspar Festival.

"The story's always the same," Marquardt said. "The treasure is buried next to a gumbo limbo tree on one of the mounds. Every year, new people hear or read those stories and they think, 'Hey—I'm going to get my buddies and do some digging.' The treasure is mythical but the hope is persistent, and it has caused a great deal of site destruction."

As has the discovery of the medallion.

"I think the whole story of the medallion is tragic," Marquardt told me. We were still at Pineland—the place that archaeologists believe is the last best hope for understanding a vanished people. We were on a bluff, looking out across a vast courtyard toward another shell pyramid. "It's tragic what happened to the boy, and it's tragic that artifact hunters have used backhoes and bulldozers to try and duplicate his find." Marquardt pointed to an old crater in the shellwork—even Pineland had not been spared. "If the medallion has a curse," he said, "you're looking at it."

A Florida Marriage

LOLA HASKINS

People think that when the Spanish named Florida they meant that the soil was full of gardens. But people were wrong. The Spanish were talking about the sky. In Florida skies, clouds are great flowers that float like hyacinths on water, burgeon, and disappear. They are misty fields whose crops wisp into the distance, as if you were passing so quickly that you couldn't quite make out what was growing and knew no more than that it might have been something to wear, soft and white and clinging to the skin. There are skies that grow flowers black as the deepest earth and these flowers swirl over your head and open, and other flowers take their place until the whole sky is black and whirling, and nothing in the sky is still. Looked at another way, you could say that clouds are Florida's mountains.

No, not Florida's mountains, because in our lifetimes mountains stay where they are, jutting up from the earth like shards or, if they are old mountains, like women's breasts. But Florida's clouds are always changing.

Stop, you say, let me get this straight. But the clouds refuse, like a child spinning in her new party dress who, as she turns, is growing up, until suddenly the white lacy skies are gone and there is only rain. And if you think that rain is rain is rain, that it's either raining or it's not, then you haven't spent much time in Florida. Here, rain is personal. Half a city gets rained on; the other half doesn't. You can stand in a field and see a curtain of water moving toward you, black as someone's feathers. Then it turns, leaving the plants at your feet desperate and wilting while a few yards away other leaves are green and perky again.

When it rains in Florida, it rains from the heart —not that all-day-gray northern drizzle, but real rain, fast and passionate, the way a child sobs, without reservation. The drops hit the ground so hard they bounce, and even harder hit the parking lots of the malls and the yellow stripes of the highways where we have paved over the land. Then lightning slashes down like the finger of God, or shoots past in a ball, or lights the whole horizon so trees appear in relief like the jagged trees of Africa. Witch-trees, the children call some of these, the leafless ones with their contorted hands, suddenly bright against the black sky.

I have a film producer friend who says that the light of each place is peculiar to itself. If you make a movie about New York and film it in Portland, the light will be wrong and any New Yorker will know it. The light in Florida is full of water. In Florida a woman's skin wrinkles more slowly—if she can stay out of the sun—because of the water. And Florida light can flood your view, fill it so completely that in the end all you see comes down to light—the way a sweet gum's leaves filter the sun and make it their own.

And implicit in any light is shadow. How many shades of gray the eye can find as it unscrambles black and white to subtle end is what looking is all about. Florida's earth is full of shadows—the tiny shades of algae floating in a swamp, the reflected shadow of a tree leaning over a river until it almost falls, the shapes of cypress roots living upwards through red lake water like the knees of hundreds of women bathing underneath, who love the lake so much they cannot leave it.

Florida's landscape is deep to love. It does not easily give itself. It's not the fish-netted high-heeled cool of a landscape that has good legs and knows it. It's a marriage, not a one-night stand, and like a marriage it rewards attention, a close look at the small things underfoot—the tiny purple flower which, held close to the eye, shows itself as orchid—or a broad look across the grasses of a prairie that notices the nuances of their arcs, the sweet blend of browns with their accents of cattail. You know such grasses by the sound of the wind shushing through their dry stalks. You can see the wind, twittering over water. In June, when most walkers stay inside, the prairie dresses itself in yellow and heartbreaking blue, and your tightening chest asks you how you could ever have stayed away. And any time of year, wherever you walk in Florida's hammocks, if you look up you will find you are canopied by the grace of Spanish moss, trailing like dancer's tulle from the oaks. If you have not lost track of your feet, you will notice the crunch of acorns as you walk, acorns with their little hats, which in a good year bring the grazing deer close in, just where you stand.

Now, if you grant that Florida is a marriage, it would be a mistake, as it would be a mistake in any long-term relationship, to think too simply. Florida is not one landscape, or even two, but a freckling of landscapes: flatwoods, hammocks of oak and magnolia, scrubland, open fields and rolling hills, swamps and rivers and lakes. And, of course, the panoramas that open to wide water—the flat Gulf Coast with its wetlands and its sand beaches white as salt, the ocean side with its sea oats and prickly pear anchoring the dunes.

And all these habitats, where we have not destroyed them, are alive with creatures that swim or fly or bound, sometimes so quickly that only an after-image tells you they were ever there. There is the fast flag of the deer, the long yellowish tail of the panther held straight behind as he runs, the tail that tells you by its thickness that this was no housecat, no feral escapee, but the real, the wild, thing. There is such wealth in Florida—a fox silver in the moon, streaking across a pasture. A rabbit in a patch of trees, hard by a possum with its white sharp grin. A crouching raccoon at dusk-time silhouetted at the high top of an oak at the edge of a clearing. And every night there are armadillos galore, with their cone-shaped snouts, trailed by hairy children whose armor is not fully plated yet.

Florida owns reptiles and amphibians to suit any fantasy, from tiny lizards that inflate the red bubbles of their throats to skinks with their thick blue and black tails. There's the ponderous gopher tortoise, too, who lives in the complicated passages of his one burrow for life. There are frogs that sit like green jewels on your windowsill or in your tub as you enter innocently to take a bath. And always, there is the alligator, sliding on his heavy belly into a tannic river or basking on the river's muddy banks. It is the eyes of alligators, hundreds of eyes just above the water, that are the lanterns of Payne's Prairie, south of Gainesville. Alligators are everywhere. They cross roads at night and linger by the hazards on golf courses—paradoxical creatures whose jaws can snap an arm at the wrist and yet are so weak that a child can hold them closed. Inside an alligator's mouth is pink light.

There are snakes. The hognose that plays cobra and if cobra should fail, goes limp and fills the air with the smell of death. But like soil under concrete, once the threat is gone, the hognose comes miraculously back to life. There is the corn snake that swallows eggs and for hours lies heavy and misshapen as each egg passes through him. There is the scarlet king, red and black and yellow, inversion of the coral snake (red, yellow, and black), a dangerous distinction for observers without an appreciation for subtlety.

There is the rattler everyone knows, the African rhythms of its body, the dancing teeth of its coils. There is the pygmy rattler, inconspicuous and overlooked, that can kill at the ankle. There is the moccasin, black and thick as a man's arm. There is the unidentifiable something that hangs from a tree as you canoe underneath.

And there are birds. Natural Florida is a paradise for birds—birds of dry grasses, birds of scrub, birds of forest, of prairie, of swamp. Birds of lakes, of rivers, of the sea. The barred owls whose sobbing wakes us up at night. The tiny flutters of sparrows, no bigger than our hearts, that settle by the hundreds on our power lines. The plain gray of a mockingbird that does not care where he is nor that it is broad daylight, but goes on pouring out his songs like milk. The osprey that flashes up from the Withlacoochee or the Ocklawaha, silver in its claws. There are ospreys, close in. They nest on telephone poles and on the light standards of baseball stadiums, within the reach of a good home run. A jogger circling an urban lake, expecting nothing, looks up and sees an osprey arrowing down from blue air.

There are bald eagles, the symbol of America. There are egrets and herons and sandhill cranes with the long legs of teenage boys that have not caught up to their bodies, sandhills who dance for each other, leaping strangely into the air, their feathers quivering, whose dances bring something to our throats. There is the anhinga, who hangs out the dark laundry of its wings. And meanwhile, overhead, the wood storks sail in wide fans, the black rims starkly elegant against white.

William Henry Hudson, the Argentinean Englishman best known for his novel *Green Mansions*, but who was also, passionately, a naturalist, had a theory that the air, even when apparently empty, is full of birds—hundreds, even thousands of birds—and that the only reason we don't see them every time we look up is that they fade into the sky, unless there is a storm. Perhaps he was thinking of wood storks or gulls. The cleanest white takes a black sky: witness the beach of a small island in the Gulf that with the light of a coming storm shines suddenly pure as sugar and you realize that though you have passed it a hundred times you have never seen it before.

Imagine a marriage in which the partners don't ever really look at each other. It happens. It's easy. A husband assumes that his wife will always be there. A wife takes her partner for granted and doesn't notice the slow changes. They grow apart. The separation is bitter.

It's the same assumption that the homesteader once made, standing on a knob in Pennsylvania under a sky dark with birds, as he knocked scores of pigeons down with a stick and strung them on his line—how can anything change? He did not notice that the migrating sky lightened year by year. He didn't think; he used. And so the divorce decree became final, and passenger pigeons disappeared forever.

Do we want that to happen here? If we are in a sense married to our Florida landscape, have we no duty of care to this partner to whom we once promised everything? Florida is delicate. She is losing her fish, her birds, the wild creatures of her woods and fields, even her plants, like the paw-paw, once so widespread. Shall we watch her fail, paler every day, and say afterwards there was nothing we could do? Not if we ever loved her. And if we care for her, we must be honest with ourselves and realize that attention is a good and a pious thing in a marriage, but it is not enough. It is not enough to write books, not enough to talk. We must save what is possible to save, what we have not already—with our talk—let go. And if we must make sacrifices to do that, so be it. Florida has given us everything, all these many years. It's our turn now.

~ ~ ~

This essay is dedicated to my father, Peter H. Behr (1915–1997), who gave his life to the preservation of the California wilderness.

Through an Open Window

RENÉE RIPPLE

The long, gray Chicago winters of my childhood fostered in me a curious and observant nature, particularly regarding anything that went on outside windows—house windows, classroom windows, car windows. I watched, face pressed against ice-cold panes of glass. When I was six or seven years old, however, the temptation to know firsthand got the better of me after the weatherman announced that, with the wind chill, the temperature outdoors was 40 degrees below zero. I bundled and wrapped and then waddled into the backyard. I stood there transfixed, momentarily blinded by snow glare. I made myself memorize the moment: the wind stinging my eyes, the cold penetrating my mittens and boots and numbing my fingertips and toes, my skin contracting inside my snowsuit. An oddity occurred then, perhaps a revelation. It still haunts me. A tiny, gray sparrow was sitting on the chain-link fence. As I turned mummy-like to get a better look, the little bird fell, solid as a rock, into the snow on our side of the fence. The nylon of my snow pants woosh-wooshed, one thigh past the other, as I hurried to the spot. The little bird, though, had disappeared.

Having lived, now, more than half of my life in Florida, my blood has warmed considerably. I watch from that special vantage that exists only outside the world's windows, still trying to memorize the many facets of this adopted landscape. My desire to transcribe experience into memory, to bear witness, has warmed as well, indeed taken on the heat of religious fervor. Every chance I get, I follow my husband, Jeff—a natural history author and landscape photographer—into the field. He, too, is a witness; his media the pen and lens. I carry gear, load Polaroid film, find the color red (he's red-green color blind). And from him, I have learned to kneel where I would have stood, to taste what I would have smelled, and to watch what I would have turned from.

At some point though, I slip away for a few minutes of private quiet, drinking in birdsong or tracing the outline of an animal track with a fingertip or pressing a cheek against weather-smoothed bark. Back in the workaday world, staring out my office window, I remember: wading waist deep in a slough in Big Cypress Swamp, watching a bald eagle devour a fish despite the intense harassment of an angry gang of jays, dancing in sweat suit and white rubber boots on a mud flat at sunset, easing my kayak up to the shoreline of Lochloosa Lake.

I collect sensory pieces, ascribe them to memory, as a hedge against tomorrow, against the ever widening torrent of development swallowing larger and larger portions of Florida's wildlands. It happens so quickly. Driving by a familiar stand of pines or remnant scrub one day, you notice a sign—Land for Sale. Weeks pass before you see it again; a corner is cleared. One house, one mobile home, a convenience store. Then, as if some unseen hand has torn down the flood gates, the land is scoured. And before long, you can't remember what was. I do not want to forget.

Lochloosa Lake is connected to Orange Lake to the southwest by Cross Creek. Much of the surrounding land—pine plantation, cow pasture, and relict hammock and cypress—has been purchased by the local water management district and/or the state. Altogether, the Lochloosa Wildlife Management Area, including lands leased by the state from timber companies, encompasses 26,637 acres. When Jeff and I, habituated to concrete and manicured lawns, first moved from south Florida to north-central Florida, we were drawn to this wild-looking area. We rented a house on Cross Creek and greeted each morning by gazing at magical, moss-draped cypress and then fell asleep at night listening to multitudes of frogs serenading one another. Before the omnipresent airboat armada chased us clear into the remnant sandhills near Williston, Lochloosa Lake introduced me to the first bald eagles I had ever seen. A resident pair nests on the lake's shore, near the mouth of the creek. Often they would fly over the Cross Creek house, heading to Orange Lake, and once we paddled our canoe as close to the nest as we thought prudent, looking up at the pair as they eyed their realm from above. I must add that keeping company with these elegant neighbors, close enough to witness firsthand their penchant for sharing roadside meals with turkey vultures, has not dulled the experience. I still get that kid-on-Christmas-morning lump in my throat every time I see one.

Three years later, kayaking on Lochloosa Lake, I had developed a more critical eye. I knew the calm surface belied the hydrilla below, its long, green tendrils choking the life out of the lake. Near shore, the hydrilla made it almost impossible to move, like drawing my paddle through wet ropes. It was so thick in some places that a moorhen, traveling toward shore, literally walked across a patch of it, unable to swim.

Jeff paddled on ahead, and I followed the moorhen to her shoreline haunts. Here cypress overhung the bank, moss dripping from boughs thirty feet up. My kayak rested, unmoving, on the massed hydrilla about four feet from the lake's edge. Huge bumblebees buzzed by on their way to flowers scattered loosely on shore. The area under the cypress was a mass of shrub and vine—a jumble of green with no way to tell where one plant ended and another began. An osprey called. Green herons darted in and out of the underbrush. The moorhen's family joined her, and they noisily foraged on shore and off. A legion of red-winged blackbirds gamboled on the branches a few feet in front of me, raucously calling and vying for space and insects. My presence seemed no cause for concern.

Mentally cataloguing the lake's amazing array of birds—snowy and great egrets, red-winged blackbirds, green and great blue herons, little blues, anhingas, osprey, and more—I closed my eyes and thought of what it must have been like to visit here long ago, before European settlement. Some say that for each bird, there would have been nine more, flying in flocks so huge they would have eclipsed the sun. Herds of deer would have paused by the lake, drinking it in, ears twitching, mindful not of scrawny, underfed hunting dogs, but of abundant black bear perhaps devouring blackberries nearby. And panther, were there ever panther here? I'm sure of it. A strong feline spirit stealthed through my vision, as real as the echoes of fish bones crushed in the jaws of river otters and the razor sharp stab of a great blue heron's beak. The very air rose and fell with the buzz and flight of all manner of insects, in turn plague and food source for multitudes of wild creatures.

During the past three years, my pilgrimages to Lochloosa Lake have revealed a place far removed from my verdant vision. Once, when driving on Lochloosa Wildlife Management Area's rutted logging roads on a cold fall day, we passed tough, free-roaming, almost malevolent looking cracker cattle. I got out, wrapped tightly in a wool shawl, to marvel at unlogged cypress, and had to step around innumerable piles of cow shit—shaped like petite termite mounds— certain to be washed into the lake with the next good rain.

Another time, a warmer day, we walked along roads worn smooth by heavy logging that had carried out much of the native longleaf and later, the spindly farmable slash pine. We saw another cow—a soft, well-bred Hereford—dead at the edge of a row of planted pine, just beginning to bloat. Nearby we found a piece of a deer's jaw bone, caressed and returned it, covering it with leaves. We stopped to count the petals of a wildflower so we could look it up later in a field guide and watched the delicate crab spider living inside. Tucked here and there under brush and wherever the logging roads intersected, heaps of garbage told an inconceivable tale of families driving miles from home, old Big Wheels and barbecue grills and car parts among the usual trash rattling in the backs of old pickup trucks. Then, like tom cats marking territory with scent, they dumped the pathetic remains of their lives, declaring their "right" to do as they please with "public" land.

Visiting the lake by kayak provided the most encompassing view. After daydreaming by the edge of the lake, I paddled out toward the center to look back at where I had been. Further on, a pair of cracker cows stood at the water's edge, contentedly pulling up huge mouthfuls of hydrilla. The drone of an airboat skating across the water toward me startled me into alertness. My kayak rocked in his wake as he passed me, heading toward shore, turning at the last second, racing under the overhanging cypress boughs. A dozen snowy egrets catapulted into hysterical flight.

I understand the futility and hopelessness espoused by some of saving this bit of ill-used Florida—preserving one stand, one flock, one herd, one anything will not bring back all that has been lost. Genetics has proved this true. On the other hand, even one tree without a logger's tag, one bird without a leg band, one panther without a radio collar, or one bear who has never seen a human preserves a window through which we can view, perhaps one day gain admittance to, where we left our souls behind.

In John Steinbeck's *Cannery Row*, the women in the brothel make a quilt. They sew together bits and pieces of worn-out lingerie and evening gowns. When I reread the book to find the passage I remembered, I found only a sentence or two, nothing more. A testament to Steinbeck's craft, for years that quilt has lived and grown in my memory—a glorious melding of colors and textures. Tattered bits of cloth sewn together, in love, into something new and beautiful and whole—a gift to soothe troubled dreams. Preservation 2000 and all such programs to acquire, preserve, and restore Florida's wildlands represent the same kind of quilting bee. Diverse members of the citizenry, each bringing a favorite piece of natural Florida and lovingly stitching it into place, into the whole.

Lochloosa Lake is one such tattered bit, logged in places, cleared in others, dumped on, beset by exotic plants, yet home to much of what is lovely and still wild. Without intervention, it could easily have dropped from our sight, like the wee sparrow. Preserved, and hopefully restored rather than "put to use," it adds much to the patchwork of Florida wildlands. It contributes its colors—the vibrant green of cypress needles in spring, the brilliant epaulettes of red-winged blackbirds, the subtle cremes and browns of its sandy soil—and its textures—skin-pricking blackberry thorns, the soft caress of myriad feathers, the smooth hardness of scattered bones. Joined together with other Florida wildlands, it represents an offering of peace to what has been lost and a declaration of hope for the future. A future where, warmed by the patchwork quilt of our own making, spirits resurrected with the flight of countless birds, lulled by frog song, and exhilarated by the rhythmic dance of predator and prey, we may sleep deeply beside an ever-open window.

The Bird and the Behemoth

ARCHIE CARR

The herons were out among the cows when I got to the prairie. I saw them first, and then I saw the dredger working.

I slowed the car to creep along, irked by the sight of the dredger, bemused for the thousandth time by egrets and cows together. Then one of the herons got up and flew in under the swooping boom and lit on the pile of mud, all white lace in the slop and splatter. He was a snowy heron, and his coming in to stand there, though a small, ill-sorted thing to see was for me a last chink stopped in a long day-dream. It was a dream of birds and behemoths and of the smallness of the world, and its essence is this: the snowy heron remembers mastodons.

Not personally, of course. I don't know how long snowy herons live. Longer than a sparrow, no doubt—less long, perhaps, than a parrot. But racially the snowy is, I'll bet, a tie with times when, faunally speaking, Florida stood shoulder to shoulder with the

Tanganyika of today. It is as plain as old bones or coprolites or rotten ivory in a Florida road-cut. Slim and impermanent as snowy herons seem, their race is old enough to recall a lot, and it does. The snowy remembers mastodons as clear as day.

Payne's Prairie is fifty square miles of level plain in north-central Florida let down in the hammock and pinelands south of Gainesville by collapse of the limestone bedrock. It drains partly into Orange Lake to the south and partly into a sinkhole at its northeast side. The sink used to clog up occasionally, and for years or decades the prairie would be under water. The people called it Alachua Lake in those times and ran steamboats on it.

Nowadays the prairie is mostly dry, with shallow ponds and patches of marsh where ancient gator holes have silted up but never disappeared, and with patches of Brahma cattle here and there out into the far spread of the plain, like antelope in Kenya. The prairie is about the best thing to see on U.S. Route 441 from the Smoky Mountains to the Keys, though to tell why would be to digress badly. But everybody with any sense is crazy about the prairie. The cowboys who work there like it and tell with zest of unlikely creatures they see—a black panther was the last I heard of—and people fish for bowfins in the ditches. There used to be great vogue in snake catching on the prairie before the roadsides became a sanctuary. People from all around used to come and catch the snakes that sunned themselves along the road shoulders. When William Bartram was there the prairie wrought him up, and his prose about the place was borrowed by Coleridge for his poem "Kubla Khan." The prairie has changed since then, with all the wolves and the Indians gone. But still there are things to make a crossing worth your while, to make it, as I said, the best two miles in all the long road south from the mountains.

I live on one side of the prairie and work on the other side. I have crossed it a thousand times. Two thousand times. And always it is something more than getting to work or going home. I have seen the cranes dance there, and a swallow-tailed kite, and on the road during one crossing, 765 snakes. And there was an early morning in October that I remember. It was after a gossamer day, a day when the spiders go ballooning in the sky. Through all the afternoon before the spiders had been flying, young spiders and old of a number of kinds, ballooning to new places in the slow flood of a southeast wind. Some of them traveled no more than ten paces, riding the pull of their hair-thin threads for the space between two bushes. Some went by a thousand feet up, streaming off to Spain on jagged white ribbons like thirty feet of spun sugar against the sky. By nightfall the whole plain was covered with the silk of all their landings. As far as you could see, the prairie was spread with a thin tissue of the dashed hopes and small triumphs of spiders, held up by the grass tips, draped over every buttonbush and willow.

We drove by in the early mist-hindered morning. The dew was down, and the drops formed strands of beads in acres of silken webbing. The fog had flaws in it here and there, and the sun coming through turned the plain all aglow, like a field of opals, and I slowed the car to look. Up toward the east from the road a Brahma bull stood in the edge of the sea of silk, and as I stopped on the shoulder across from where he was he raised his head to look our way. He was stern and high-horned and stood straight up from the forequarters, like an all-bull centaur. Suddenly the sunlight touched him and my wife and I fell to beating at each other, each to be first to say: "Look at his horns." The old bull had gone grazing in the night, and now his horns were all cross-laced with silk picked up from the grass. He stood there with the sun rising behind him, and his horns were like a tall lyre strung with strings of seed pearls gathered in the mist and burning in the slanted light.

There is no telling the things you see on the prairie. To a taste not too dependent upon towns, there is always something, if only a new set of shades in the grass and sky or a round-tail muskrat bouncing across the blacktop or a string of teal running low with the clouds in the twilight in front of a winter wind. The prairie is a solid thing to hold to in a world all broken out with man. There is peace out there, and quiet to hear rails call and cranes bugling in the sky.

I slowed down, as I said at the start, just to watch the egrets with the cattle and to fret at the mess the dredge was making, sloshing about the old ditch, slinging muck about, scaring the cooters and congo eels. It was a big diesel dragline, a Lorraine 81. It was scooping fill for another pair of road lanes. It crouched in the muck on caterpillar tracks, and the steel boom that held the bucket up slanted away for sixty feet against the sky. In the shiny yellow cab a fat man snatched and shoved at a row of levers, barely able, it seemed to me, to keep up with the churning rhythm he was making. It was imposing, in the way of ponderous engines, the big, live-looking thing turning on the groaning bull gear, casting the brutal jaw, horsing up six-yard mouthfuls of spouting muck, and twisting to drop them on the growing fill. It was a gross, unlikely thing to see, a metal behemoth sloshed out to wreck the plain in vast quest of Mesozoic tubers.

It was that sort of fanciful thinking that slowed me down. But as I started to crawl on by, the egret left his cow and came flying in to the dragline. Straight in under the swinging tower it flew, and it lit on the piled new muck. I quickly looked up and down the road for a bump on a black and tan car that would mean a state trooper was coming. Seeing none, I pulled out onto the grass shoulder and shut the engine off.

I was only thirty feet from where the heron was, but it paid no heed to my being there. Its mind was all taken up with the fine things the dragline was spilling. Each time the bucket sucked out and rose, there seemed no way the heron could keep clear of the spilling mud. Each time the bucket dropped I looked for it to paste the bird flat with the splash. But always it jumped easily away and back again and fell to jabbing about and throwing its head up to juggle some squirming little animal and swallow it with hurried zest. Close in to the clamor and race of the engine, to the slap of cables and chains and chatter of drums and sheaves, it worked away, completely single-minded in its gleaning. Drag, hoist, twist, drop, twist, cast, drag; and the egret flapped in under the soaring bucket and took up the sad, succulent creatures from the mud, out of the midst of their disaster.

For a time I watched as if watching any unmeaning oddity. Then I caught a quick smell of half-burnt diesel fuel, and it took me back, the way odors sometimes do, to the deck of the *Piri Piri* on the Zambezi River and the smell in the air of a hot African afternoon, and to a flock of white herons standing on another plain with cows. Thinking about it in time and space like that, I saw all at once that a change had blurred the form of the dragline by the road. A sort of flesh seemed to be filling out the steel bones of the engine, and before my eyes it took a fleeting mammal form—not solid skinbound shape, you know, but an eerie, momentary show of creature stuff partly condensed about the metal frame. You can't think how weird it was. It made me look hard; and after a bit I seemed to make out in the mist, still working away, still sloshing about in the ditch, the form of an old bull mastodon.

It was only for a moment. Then a car went by, headed south. The driver glanced the way I was looking but quickly turned back to visions of his own, to whatever draws the Yankee down to the end of Route 441. That made it plain that I was seeing untrustworthy things, and I looked back, and sure enough, the elephant had all ebbed away. The dredge was working for what it was, the motor straining at the drag chains and chattering through the turns, the steel mouth gnashing the muck to froth. But short as the stay of the elephant had been, it made sense of the heron's presence there.

When I moved to Florida the herons were wading birds. The cattle roamed the unfenced woods or sloshed about wet prairies—puhraries, the Crackers called them—the marshes of maidencane, bonnets, and pickerelweed. The herons stayed in what you think of as heron habitat, in the shallow lakes and pond edges, and along the roadside ditches. They ate frogs and fishes there and little snakes and sirens. Even in those days there was a big cattle industry in Florida, but it was the hit-and-miss husbandry of the old Spaniards, profitable mainly because the stock was as Spartan as camels and land was cheap.

Then all at once the land began to change. A new sort of ranching grew up, with fences and purebred stock and planted pastures. New breeds were coddled in stumped-out, smoothed-over lands. The hammocks were cleared of brush and the palmettos were bulldozed away to make the flatwoods into parks. Patrician Angus, Hereford, and Indian bulls were sent out to serve the skittish Spanish she-stuff, and pretty soon, all over northern Florida, fat cows were being gentled on a new kind of tended lawn. By the thousands of acres the old rough land that no sane heron would be caught dead in was made into pangola parkland and clover savanna, into manmade pampa and veld of Bahia and napier grass. It was a landscape made over; and as strange as the change in the land itself was the change in the ways of the snowy heron.

To see what lured the heron ashore you have to understand that every Florida rancher, in spite of his dreams and all the courses he had in the College of Agriculture, is not likely ever to find himself raising cattle in pure culture. He will inevitably turn out to be a grasshopper husbandman as well. In fact, if he should stock his pastures with just the right number of cows, a number that eats grass exactly as fast as the grass replaces itself, a certain predictable yearly crop can be harvested. Of course, no rancher in his right mind works that way. He pieces out the winter diet of his cattle with protein and minerals and moves them to winter oats, and he does all he can to supplement the basic productivity of the pasture grass. But if only swamps have dried into forest and then into chaparral, and then through slow millennia have become swamps again. But even with all this going on the snowy would only have to shift his ways a little to survive—this way in the times when the fishes flourished, that way when the frogs became mummies in the cracking mud.

When the pterodactyls, the flying reptiles, mysteriously quit the world for good in the late Cretaceous, there were aspirant bats to fit the living space they left. When dinosaurs dissolved away during the same calamitous times, mammals were on hand to take over their roles and skills and to think up many more besides. But in the more recent great extinction, that of the Ice Age grassland fauna, there has been only the most spurious replacement of what was lost. A whole life-form has dropped out of the old land-life structures. Throughout North America the whole grazing-browsing savanna community is gone or going. There is a rent-out space in the life web where only a little while ago five kinds of elephants—and camels and horse, bison and shrub oxen, pronghorns, and cervid deer—were making mammal landscapes that, you can see in even the dim evidence of bones, were the equal of any the world has known. It was in northern and central Florida that the great savanna fauna probably persisted the longest. Paleoecologists now say it might have held on down to no more than four thousand to eight thousand years ago. It has been no time at all since the animals were here when you think about how wholly they are gone, how empty of them the days are under the same sun and rain, how recently their horn flies dwindled, the condors mourned over the last cadavers, and the dung beetles turned to quibbling over piles of rabbit pills.

And back at home you come upon a raging dragline with a wisp of a snowy heron there dodging the cast and drop of the bucket as if only mammoth tusks were swinging—and what can it be but a sign of lost days and lost hosts that the genes of the bird remember?

perennial grasses supported his cows, there would be in the pasture a certain fixed ration of grass to meat.

Well, it's the same with his grasshopper culture. Let the insects move in and breed and live there with the cattle—and there is no way to keep them out—and the weight of the insect meat will be predictable too. The awful part is, it may not be a whole lot less than the weight of the beef. The herons of course know nothing of the rules of physiological ecology that make this so. But they know a good thing when they see it. And during the time between the two world wars, the snowy egret in northern Florida changed from merely a water bird to a seasonally insectivorous associate of cows.

When I first began to notice snowy egrets walking with cows the birds were with black cows mostly, and the two together were a fancy thing to see. I got into a great state of excitement; and knowing no ornithologist in those days, I canvassed the cattlemen of the county to see what they could tell me. Without exception they had noticed the hegira of the herons, and they dated it as "just lately"—lately being the early 1930s. When I went on to quiz them further, some said it was the coming of the Angus cattle that drew the birds ashore, some queer attraction of Angus black for egret white. But those with a less mystical cast of mind said it was not the blackness of the cows at all but the pastures smoothed out in the old rough hammock and palmetto land, the brand new bowling green laid out for a stick-legged wading bird to walk in. I looked through the bird books I could find and from them went to journals. Always the snowy was cited as a water bird—one who is more active in his hunting than the rest—but never a cattle heron. Before the 1930s nobody spoke of snowy herons walking with cattle. By the end of the thirties they were observed doing it all over the place.

Looking back to those times you can see that several changes favored the hegira of the herons. These were the years when egrets were making their great comeback after plume hunting had reduced them almost to extinction at the turn of the century. And the new flocks were not surging back into the old Florida but into a land less fit for herons, with marshes and gladeland everywhere being drained and made into farms or real estate. Then there were the new crops of grazing grasshoppers on dry land, fed upon teeming tons on clear stands of planted grass, and there were placid cattle there to stir them out of hiding. And as important as any part of the new outlook was the change from the cluttered hammock and palmetto pinelands to lawns of short grass as wadeable to heron legs as water.

Traces of the sort of mind it takes to go ashore and consort with behemoths can be seen in the snowy heron's relatives. But in them the venture has the look of aberrant behavior of a timid, unhappy straying from the comfort of the normal. The snowies, however, came out in confident flocks from the start. They emerged with unawed enthusiasm, as if loosed at last among joys once known and too long withheld from their bloodline. So nowadays the cattle quarter the mankept plains, the grasshoppers fly up and the snowies snatch them out of the air. It was a rare thing they found, a feeding niche not occupied, a chance going begging. Any frog-spiking heron has the eye and the tools to tweak down a grasshopper out of the air, but only the snowy had the wit and the gall to out and do it.

But wit and gall—what do they mean in a heron? What trait of mind was it really, that singled out the snowy among his fellows and let him go out and use cows to harvest the new manna in the new landscape? Where did the flexibility come from? Why was the snowy so much the most ready when the new opportunity came along?

I think I know. I think they got inured to behemoths by walking with the fauna of the Pleistocene. Through millions of years Florida was spread with veld or tree savanna. Right there in the middle of Payne's Prairie itself there used to be creatures that would stand your hair on end. Pachyderms vaster than any now alive grazed the tall brakes or pruned the thin-spread trees. There were llamas and camels of half a dozen kinds; and bison and sloths and glyptodonts; bands of ancestral horses; and grazing tortoises as big as the bulls. And all these were scaring up grasshoppers in numbers bound to make a heron drool. Any heron going out among those big mammals—any small white bird able to make use of a glyptodont to flush his game—would have to have guts galore and a flexible outlook; but he would get victuals in volume.

Back among the ice ages and before, there must have been times, thousands of years at a stretch, when marshes and swamps went slowly dry, and frogs and puddle fishes grew scarce. At times like those the crotchbound kinds of herons could only mope and squabble about the dwindling water holes and starve there or go away some place. But any heron strain with even a mite of extra flexibility would not need many generations to work out a way to live out in the grass.

Grasshoppers are hard to see, for a man at least, and I daresay for a heron too. They are colored all wrong to be seen, for one thing; and they have an unfair way of circling a stem of grass and sneering at you from off side. But it is different when you walk down close to the nose of a cow. Out in front of a cow the grasshoppers are unable to use their cunning. They have to spew out into the clear like quail flushing ahead of a crazy setter. And for a fish-fast, frog-quick heron, picking them out of the air on the rise is no trick at all. The only hard part would be daring to move in close to the head of a creature a thousand times your size, the restringing of thin herons' nerves for consorting with behemoths—with cattle or mammoths or draglines.

There is no telling when the snowy's nerves were restrung— maybe as far back as the Pliocene, maybe further. In terms of a geological time, climate has always been unsettled, and animals have changed with the climate or gone away or simply died. Again and again marsh has baked into adobe plain, tadpoles have withered,

Islands in Time

DON STAP

On a sunny day in March 1992, John Fitzpatrick, then the director of Archbold Biological Station in Lake Placid, Florida, took me for a drive to show me a tract of Florida scrub, an ecosystem estimated to be two million years old. Pulling off the highway at the edge of a citrus grove near the station, Fitzpatrick plowed up a slope of fine, white sand in his four-wheel-drive Bronco. Bouncing and twisting, we ascended a hill that rose to 150 feet, about as great an uprising as one can find in Florida. At the top of the ridge, we got out and walked a few steps into a patchwork of stunted, gnarled vegetation that indeed looked ancient. The twisted trunks of saw palmettos, which grew as much horizontally as vertically, appeared wilted, barely able to rise off the ground; dwarf oaks, whose thick leaves had curled like dried leather under the Florida sun, were no more than five or six feet tall.

Though the oaks grew in formidable thickets, there were also open patches of bare sand and, in places, clumps of prickly pear cactus. Under the late winter sun, the dull, overlapping greens of the scrub resembled that confusing section of the jigsaw puzzle one leaves for last. The only outstanding feature was the few scattered pine trees that dominated the landscape, their straight trunks rising branchless forty feet or more before blossoming into evergreen crowns. The miniature forest beneath the pines looked as barren as living matter can appear.

When early travelers through Florida came upon an expanse of the prickly, inhospitable scrub, they saw a wasteland. One visitor wrote: "These tracts [of scrub] are, in fact, concealed deserts, as they are too poor to admit of cultivation, and afford nothing that is fit, even for the browsing of cattle." A later visitor observed that scrub "appears to desire to display the result of the misery through which it has passed and is passing in its solution to life's grim riddle."

A grim riddle is how it seemed on that day in 1992. Although an astounding 40 percent of the plants found in scrub are endemic to it (eleven plants are federally listed as endangered, two as threatened, and thirteen more are on the waiting list), these dry uplands—the oldest ecosystem in the Southeast—were disappearing probably faster than any other habitat in the United States. Approximately 85 percent of Florida's original scrub has been destroyed.

Only moments earlier on the way to this site, we had stopped on the side of the road and Fitzpatrick pointed out my window to what he called "The Moonscape": 1,600 acres of bare sand. There, several years earlier, a citrus grower and developer had scraped bare what had been the largest privately owned, untouched tract of scrub in the state. When Fitzpatrick first drove out to look at the damage, he found scrub jays, a species that lives only in scrub, perched on all that remained of their home: the bulldozed piles of uprooted trees. The jays had nowhere to go and would die slowly over the next few months. All of the remaining Florida scrub in the area was already filled to capacity by jay families that would vigorously defend their territories.

That anything lives in scrub is a testament to the efficacy of evolution. The conditions of Florida scrub are extreme, and paradoxical. Although Florida summers are hot and humid, dominated by intense afternoon thundershowers, and the annual rainfall averages fifty inches, scrub is a desert habitat: rain drains quickly through the fine sand as if through a sieve. Even though Fitzpatrick was pointing out to me the features of the scrub immediately before us, I found it difficult to see the forest for the trees, which looked to me like a bonsai garden gone to seed. In scrub, people become giants, their heads poking out above the treetops.

"You have to get down on your hands and knees and look at it from a gopher tortoise's point of view," Fitzpatrick likes to say. Many plants grow only a few inches high, producing bouquets of flowers fit for a doll's house, and the only evidence of many scrub animals is an entrance to a burrow.

The inhabitants of scrub are often as peculiar as they are diminutive: the short-tailed snake has no known relatives and no fossil record; the scrub firefly flies in daylight; and the rare sand skink, a legless lizard, rarely sees the light of day, preferring to spend its time beneath the sand where it swims fish-fashion in pursuit of its prey— termites and beetle larvae.

Scrub is also home to many Florida animals whose numbers are diminishing throughout the state, including the red-cockaded woodpecker, sandhill crane, Bachman's sparrow, Eastern indigo snake, blue-tailed mole skink, Florida black bear, fox squirrel, and, the state's rarest mammal, the Florida panther. Looking around, Fitzpatrick smiled faintly. "Here they are, some of the rarest plants in the world, all within an arm's reach of each other."

Now, Fitzpatrick stood up and spread his arms wide. "People say,

'You want to save everything.' No, we don't, I tell them. We just want to save what's left—the crumbs of the pie so we can smell them and imagine what the whole pie must have been like."

From the ridge top, we could look out on what had become of the pie. Turning 360 degrees, I saw nothing but orange trees running in every direction as far as I could see. Within my view were roughly four million orange trees, worth, at their maturity, $21 million in net profit annually. Much of Florida's citrus industry moved south to Highlands County, where most of the remaining scrub is located, after several freezes in the 1980s destroyed many of the Orlando area groves 100 miles to the north. Citrus growers prefer Highlands County not only because damaging freezes are highly unlikely, but because the county is aptly named: it is *high land* and orange trees grow best in well-drained soil like the fine "sugar sand" found in scrub. This sand is the key to the origin of scrub. Where Fitzpatrick and I stood it was more than 150 feet deep. We were, in fact, atop a sand dune formed millions of years ago when the Atlantic Ocean— presently sixty miles to the east—would have been lapping the beach little more than a stone's throw from us.

The Florida peninsula is a recent addition to North America, appearing above water for the first time about twenty-five million years ago when sea levels worldwide fell dramatically. Since then, the seas have risen and fallen several times, most recently during the glacial intervals of the Pleistocene. During those high sea level periods when the peninsula was only a few miles wide, wave action piled up sand dunes, which, when the seas receded to their present level, left a high ridge that runs down the center of the peninsula. When the water level was particularly high, the uppermost points on the Florida ridge became an archipelago of islands in a shallow sea on which evolved species unique to their own isolated habitat. Today, these sandy islands, like the one Fitzpatrick and I stood on, are surrounded by a sea of orange groves and housing developments.

A major section of this sandy spine, known as the Lake Wales Ridge, extends southward from an area just west of Orlando to the southern boundary of Highlands County. Roughly a hundred miles long and four to ten miles wide, this ridge holds a large portion of the extant scrub in the state. Scientists have determined that of 200,000 original acres of scrub on the Lake Wales Ridge system, fewer than 20,000 acres of the unique scrub remain. In the 1980s, federal and state agencies, in concert with Archbold and The Nature Conservancy, put together a proposal that would protect 10,000 acres on twelve separate sites as a national wildlife refuge. During my first visit to the area, the refuge was only in the planning stage, and Fitzpatrick was worried that more scrub would be developed before money was appropriated to purchase it for preservation.

A few weeks after my visit with Fitzpatrick, I returned to Archbold just in time to watch twenty-eight acres of scrub go up in flames. A billowing plume of white smoke was rising into the sky as I drove up to the headquarters. Moments later I was escorted to the front line of the fire, where I met up with Eric Menges, Archbold's resident botanist. Menges, a man whose friendliness is hidden behind a serious expression and a bushy beard, stood beside a four-wheel-drive vehicle, hastily eating a peanut butter and jelly sandwich.

"We just started," he told me, pointing toward a strip of scrub still smoldering from the fire that had raced through it.

For tens of thousands of years, before settlers cleared Florida's extensive pine forests and modern firefighters extinguished blazes that threatened homes and citrus groves, forest fires repeatedly ravaged the state's dry uplands. The fires were frequent—Florida averages more ground flashes from lightning than any place else in the United States—and, consequently, the scrub ecosystem evolved as a pyrogenic community: plants and animals alike adapted to the recurring catastrophe of forest fires. As a result, fire is as essential to the long-term health of scrub as rainfall. To re-create what once was natural, Eric Menges burns off selected sites of overgrown scrub each year according to a carefully plotted master plan.

Without these frequent fires, the elfin woodland becomes so dense it chokes out virtually all undergrowth, leaving none of the grasses and other plants that gopher tortoises, white-tailed deer, the endangered Florida mouse, and other scrub inhabitants depend on for food. In addition, the oaks of overgrown scrub stop producing enough acorns for scrub jays, and the spreading trees cover up the sandy patches where jays would hide them. In fact, the presence of scrub jays is a sure sign of healthy scrub. Their absence, as was the case in the scrub Menges was burning off, indicated scrub that was unnaturally overgrown.

On this day, Menges had selected a twenty-eight-acre tract of scrub that had not burned, he estimated, since the 1920s. Because overgrown scrub such as this is dense, as well as extremely dry and filled with branches just the right size for kindling, it creates a spectacular fire that races through it quickly. As Menges spoke, we could hear the fire coming our way. We had reached a point where a spur of burned off scrub lay behind us. A hundred feet ahead of us we could see plumes of black and white smoke rising swiftly, then mushrooming two hundred feet into the air. Seventy-foot pine trees swayed and shook in the thermal updrafts. The fire climbed them in a matter of seconds, engulfing the crowns all at once. In an instant the cones of the sand pines glowed red, lighting up like Christmas tree lights.

As the fire approached to within thirty feet, it felt like a hot iron pressed against my chest. We began to back up. The palmetto fronds before us crackled and sizzled, disintegrating from the heat even before the flames reached them. Menges gestured to the blackened area behind us. The roar of the fire, like a sheet of metal being whipped back and forth, made conversation nearly impossible. We stepped back into the safety of the burned out scrub behind us. Then the seventy-foot tidal wave of flame coming at us hit a wall of nothing and fell to the foot of the last oaks. A cactus contorted in the intense heat, slumping to the ground like a deflated balloon.

Later, looking at the remains of the fire, I found it hard to think of this as "habitat restoration." The trunks of the pines were scorched black, their bark reduced to charcoal. The dwarf oaks were leafless skeletons. All that remained of the palmettos were the clustered trunks, which looked like the contorted arms of a dying octopus. Here and there white smoke rose from the smoldering duff. Everything was covered with black ash—the negative of a winter scene—and the acrid smell of burnt wood hung in the air. I could not imagine a more desolate landscape.

Nevertheless, many of the scrub plants, which appear devastated by a fire, have evolved remarkable means to survive. The tall sand pines hold great clusters of cones that usually remain on the tree for years, opening only in response to the 400°F heat of a fire. Their seeds then fill the air in the days following a fire, ensuring survival of the species. The dwarf oaks maintain 75 percent of their biomass safely beneath the sand in the form of underground networks of rhizomes, rootlike horizontal stems that send new sprouts upward. Perhaps most amazing of all among the pyrogenically adapted plants is Florida rosemary, which releases a chemical into the soil around it apparently to stop its own seeds from germinating. The seeds remain in the soil and do not sprout until a fire kills off the mother plant.

In May 1993, almost exactly a year later, I visited Archbold once again. I was curious to see what the previous year's burn site looked like, and I wondered also what progress had been made on the Lake Wales Ridge National Wildlife Refuge. Had the state or federal government purchased any land during the last year, I asked Fitzpatrick. "No," he answered bluntly. "Not a bit." Fitzpatrick was unhappy with how slowly the rusty wheels of bureaucracy were turning. A year later, however, he would report that a particularly important 3,000-acre tract of scrub had been purchased, and other acquisitions looked promising.

Later that day I walked through the previous year's burn site with Eric Menges. Menges pointed out some of the new growth. Cutthroat grass carpeted the area. The palmettos were once again green, and oak seedlings were growing profusely nearly everywhere we stepped. Several plants were flowering: slender blazing star, St. John's wort, and tarflower. Scrub blueberry, which bears fruit only the first few years after a fire, was flourishing as well. We picked a few of the ripened berries, not much bigger than peppercorns, and not much sweeter.

Animals too had moved back into the area. We scared up a pair of ground doves as we walked, and I could hear a towhee calling—then, somewhere in the distance, a great-crested flycatcher. I stopped a moment to watch two red-bellied woodpeckers circle a dead pine tree. In two more years, maybe three, the oaks would bear acorns again, and a family of scrub jays would move into the area, staking out a new territory amidst the austere beauty of this timeworn forest.

A Life in the Scrub

AL BURT

While walking a trail through the woods to our mailbox, something brushed against my leg. Looking down, I saw an agitated coral snake butting its head into my khaki pants. I had stepped on some leaves and it popped out, protesting. The candy-striped body attacked but the tiny mouth could not deliver its poison, deadly enough to cripple or kill a slow walker like me before I could get back to the house. No damage done, to that usually lethargic beauty or to me, just a speculative shock. In such small, everyday ways the scrub demands attention from those who live there.

In tourist-oriented Florida, the scrub has the character of a geographic dinosaur, scattered about in bone-dry islands on a generally green and wet peninsula. Its environment affects all life it touches, imposing limitations in exchange for opportunities rarely appreciated except by contrarians and old-time Floridians. About it there is an ugly duckling quality that takes on truth and beauty in the eyes of certain beholders.

Among the gentle sandhills and clear lakes that put marks of grace and greenery on the fringe of scrub where I live, along two-rut roads (like my driveway) that cut through what is left of these ancient dune deserts, that peculiar beauty thrives with quiet drama. Nearly all its creatures struggle for life in varying degrees of desperation. You cannot be gulled by illusions of Florida as Eden and exist happily in the scrub country. This is Florida with a full set of thorns, native Florida that glories in its blemished jewels, not cosmetized, not hidden behind exotic facades that mimic some other place. Here you can see what Florida looked like before it sold its soul to the tourists.

Naturally, tourists, in their ignorance, avoid it, adding reason to sentiment why many old-timers embrace the scrub's bittersweet flavors. Bugs, crawly things and enhanced summer humidity disguise its homegrown sweetness. Joys tend to be earthy, maybe a little itchy; a range of irritations sharpen the contrarian philosophy and awaken the survival instincts. Even a walk to the mailbox carries an underlining of curiosity about undetected wonders in familiar places, sensitizing the mind to small joys—the gift of deep-hued wildflowers, the relief of a true spring and fall, the call and rustle of wild things, the exhilaration of walking under tall trees and across unbroken land—and generating childlike awe. The scrub exaggerates its own mystery and delivers a natural high.

Strangers enjoy hearing tales about such things as coral snakes. These provide logic for their distaste and confirm prejudice. Most of us who live in or about the scrub do what we can to perpetuate that. My all-time favorite snake tale involved a remote, woodsy retreat where I spent many good summer days in my youth. The house sat by a small lake. To get there, our car had to grind across three miles of a deep-rutted sand trail that dodged among tall pine trees. Since the 1920s, the place had been a vacation retreat, unoccupied except for brief periods. Wildlife, prominently including Florida's full range of snakes, owned it most of the time. I can remember encounters with rattlesnakes longer than I was. They coiled under the palmettos, sunned on logs, prowled flower beds, their rattles held high and rasping like soft castanets. They were kings on the ground.

The coral snakes, by contrast, were quiet and sneaky despite their striped brightness. This one story I remember especially. The elders went to bed early. Nighttime there was total black, broken only by fireflies and stars and the moon, given sound only by a few birds, the stamping of deer by the lake, leaves stirred by a curious raccoon, or an acorn dropping and rattling loudly down the tin roof. So the sound of a woman's poorly stifled scream resounded dramatically. A coral snake had entered the bedroom and snuggled into the light bedcovers. When the covers were moved, it wriggled too close. Forever after, all of us slept lightly in that house, paying proper homage to the powers of the scrub.

Definitions of the scrub have become looser and varied as it disappears before development but, for me, the scrub is old Florida. As sea levels fell during the Ice Ages, Florida rose up out of the water. Tides turned the old ocean bottom into dunes or irregular ridges. Wind and time turned some of those into graceful sandhills with stunted, scraggly vegetation so persistent it could exist on almost nothing but still so delicate that even a footstep might damage it. What some consider the best parts of the scrub, in particular the dune ridge down the Florida east coast which the railroad favored, have been killed with kindness. Developers showered that high ground with water and fertilizer and out of the sterile sand sprouted grass and shrubs, turning pale earth colors into splashes of green. Except for a few spots carefully preserved, either through neglect or design, the scrub survived mostly in the interior, often in patches or islands. Years of Florida rain, growth, and decay altered even those.

My piece of the scrub (altitude 180 feet) in north-central Florida near Melrose where I have lived the last quarter-century—not far from where I vacationed as a boy—underwent the same changes. Greenery rings the many lakes that dot the landscape, and development pokes long green fingers into the scrub. Deep, infertile sand underlies almost all. It is difficult to walk on anytime but near impossible for bare feet in the summer, when the sand gets hot enough to blister the soles. The best of the scrub survives in large private holdings, in institutional retreats or in preserves created to study what wildlife and natural vegetation were like in the original Florida. The lucky setting for my home, six acres in a live oak grove on a clear lake, enjoys proximity to all three of those and therefore has a window on the scrub.

The original roads in our area were created as explorers from Gainesville and Jacksonville drove cross-country to get to the lakes. Pioneering drivers simply chose the paths most free of obstacles. Wherever the tires touched, near-permanent tracks were laid. Repetitious crossings created deep ruts where tires mired up in white sand. Some of those roads later were paved, but many of the rutted ones remain. Even today, if a delivery or repairman's truck ventures carelessly out of the ruts in my driveway, a track is laid that will remain for years. In the scrub's fragile vegetation, scars last a long time.

Live oak groves like mine also scatter across this countryside, creating other oases among the scrub's scraggly growth, among the small blackjack or turkey oaks, Christmas-shaped sand pines as well as the tall slash pines, rosemary bushes, saw palmettos, any number of dwarfed plants that manage to glean life out of the deep sand and harshly dry conditions. Fox squirrels, gopher tortoises, armadillos, raccoons, possums, deer, and bobcats roam the area where we two-legged ones intrude. Great varieties of songbirds put color and sound into the trees, and woodpeckers, including the giant pileated, peck away at the dead trees. Buzzards ride the thermal currents and feast on road kills or other victims.

In winter the smell of wood smoke from house chimneys perfumes the air. Gopher tortoises dig mysterious-looking dens, sometimes taken over by rattlesnakes. Expectant tortoises lumber out and scratch depressions into the sand to lay their eggs where they will hatch in the hot sun. Sensitive residents erect markers to protect the tortoise nests. One neighbor daubed a bit of blue paint on a tortoise shell so he could keep informal check on its welfare. Another mounted a squirrel blind and stood guard with a .22 rifle to keep squirrels from gnawing the wood and punching holes in the screen on his porch. Armadillos root up the yards. Once, after observing an armadillo rooting up my small stand of lakeside grass, I ambled out to it on my walking cane. It was so intent it paid no attention to me. Trying to save my grass, I rapped it lightly on the back with my cane, supposing that I could scare it off. The thing leaped up so fiercely I thought I was being attacked. I left and let it eat. A fox and a possum compete at our dogs' feed bowl at night. During winter, especially, deer come tripping out of the scrub to nibble at our green plantings. We feed them cracked corn in an effort to save the shrubs.

Planting in the sand is a challenge and we are protective. Anything but native plants is a mistake. To get them started, even they require peat and mulch to keep the rainwater from leaching quickly through, plus gentle fertilizers that won't damage their delicate roots. Once they are established, you can relax.

Raccoons regularly raid the bird feeder. One night two exotic looking cats (perhaps bobcats, but they looked larger and had long tails) took over our circled driveway. We gave them lots of room. A large pine snake crawled up into the azalea by our bedroom window and ate a songbird out of its nest. It was like watching horror television.

Egrets and ibises and great blue herons stalk the edge of the lake. Bass and bream swirl the waters. Occasionally, alligators float out just beyond our swimming area and act as lifeguards. Once, during mating season, a gator roared like an angry dinosaur and cavorted about on top of the water in a fascinating scene. Eagles soar over, looking for ducks or other small animals. Lightning cracks into our woods, sometimes taking down trees or television aerials. High winds in the summer thunderstorms can skip unmanned boats across the lake like small stones. Lake levels rise and fall with the rain, but during the 1990s mostly fell, whatever the rainfall.

As I see them, at least, those who choose a life in the scrub identify themselves by the choice. Like the animals and the vegetation, they have mixed qualities of beauty and frailty. Their variety is as infinite as the scrub where they live but some tendencies show. They like elbow room, tend to be a bit reclusive, respond well to kind treatment but scare easily and scratch back if abused. Like the coral snake, they are tolerant, but approach them with caution: they have poison even though it is rarely delivered.

Area folk may be more restrained by custom than law. History gets more honor than fashion and recognition more than change. Neighbors, it seems to me, enjoy visiting the tourist spots and the crowded haunts along the beaches the way city folk enjoy going to the zoo. They like to feed the monkeys and observe the exotics. It would not be right for the scrub, but it has entertainment value. Most are the kind of folk who either go to church on Sunday or respect those who do. Neighbors support each other with a fervor that suggests they fully believe themselves to be piling up credits in heaven. In our time, the area has suffered break-ins, a marijuana bust, a moonshine raid that recovered a stolen dumpster that had been converted into a still, a murder plot. Life goes on as in the cities, but still there is a sense that something special exists here. We rationalize the bad things as exceptions and, of course, they are.

The Sweet Scent of Pinewoods at Dawn

JEFF RIPPLE

*We left the magnificent savanna and its delightful groves,
passing through a level, open, airy pine forest, the stately
trees scatteringly planted by nature, arising straight and
erect from the green carpet, embellished with various
grasses and flowering plants . . . which continued for many
miles, never out of sight of little lakes or ponds . . .*
WILLIAM BARTRAM, *Travels of William Bartram*

Not far from my home is a forest, an extraordinary forest, that I visit often. I don't consider it extraordinary so much for its heart-wrenching beauty—some people might even think it plain—but rather for what it represents. It is a remnant of a landscape that once covered much of the southern United States and now is nearly gone.

Only three hundred years ago, vast forests of longleaf pine reached from the Atlantic Ocean to the Gulf of Mexico, covering eighty million acres, including parts of Virginia, the Carolinas, Georgia, Florida, Alabama, Mississippi, and Texas. Some seventy million of those acres were pure stands in which wire grass and a diverse assemblage of wildflowers and other herbaceous plants tossed and waved like a restless sea beneath the pine canopy. Fires, typically caused by lightning, were frequent and blazed for miles and miles, burning away undergrowth without killing the pines, leaving bare soil from which new longleaf seedlings sprouted and soft, new wire-grass surged forth.

Three hundred years is not such a long time. A longleaf pine may live for three hundred years or more. To think that within the life-time of a single tree, we have changed unalterably the face of the landscape it knew as a seedling.

From the period immediately after the Revolutionary War through the first decade of the twentieth century, longleaf pine—also called Georgia pine, southern yellow, long needle, and long straw—was relentlessly timbered and its gummy resin used for tur-pentine, tar, pitch, and rosin or "navy stores." Virtually all virgin longleaf had been cut by 1930. Of the original eighty million acres of longleaf, about three million acres now remain, most of which is second growth and degraded by grazing, logging, and lack of fire. Only isolated groves of virgin longleaf remain, a thousand acres or so. A few of those grand, old trees, somehow missed by loggers, stand in this woodland I visit so often—Goethe State Forest.

Goethe would have been insignificant in that once vast southern forest. Now it represents some of the best pine country left any-where, covering sixty-six square miles in southeastern Levy County, extending from a point three miles north of the Withlacoochee River to just below the city of Bronson. It stretches a modest six miles at its widest point, but runs roughly twenty miles from north to south. Goethe is cloaked predominantly with longleaf and slash pines, inter-woven with swatches of hammock, freshwater marsh, and cypress swamp. From its wetlands spring innumerable creeks and the headwaters of the Wekiva River. Longleaf pine and turkey oak sandhill saddle its northern reaches, where the land is slightly higher and much drier and cradles small, sometimes ephemeral, lakes within.

Goethe also harbors several uncommon life forms—Florida black bear, red-cockaded woodpecker, indigo snake, gopher tortoise, kestrel, southern bald eagle, Sherman's fox squirrel, corkwood, pinewood dainty. Deer, of course, are plentiful, as are bobcats, gray squirrels, wild turkey, and other plants and wildlife no less significant to a woodland than those listed under the heading of Endangered or Threatened Species in Goethe State Forest's Resource Management Plan. It's just that in these days of rapidly diminishing wilderness, what is rare gets attention. The less we have of something—a dainty, a fox squirrel, a longleaf pine forest—the more precious it is to us. Hence, Goethe.

I visit these woods for varied reasons, no one more significant than another. Sometimes I hike or write. Sometimes I sit on a favorite log and watch the morning light play in the trees and clouds. More often, I bring my wooden field camera and photograph. With the camera in my hands I creep along and listen to the forest. I intuit the dance of shadow and light, the pitch and form of trees, the texture of bark and grass and leaves. I wait for the forest to tell me in my gut what I will photograph. When it has spoken, when I settle the camera on the tripod and peer through the ground glass, I feel my body drawn through the lens and swallowed by the landscape before me. I become what I see.

Perhaps that is so with others who enter the forest—hikers, hunters, biologists, birders. I hope so, because it is they—us—who must speak for this forest, any forest, in the community and in government. Not everyone cares about endangered species or the sweet scent of a pinewoods at dawn. The spiritual qualities of a wildland and its inhabitants are often overshadowed by economics, the bottom line: "Tell me how much this forest is worth in dollars and cents." An international corps of economists, ecologists, and policy analysts did so, in terms of the earth's natural systems as a whole and the myriad ways they aid humankind, in the science journal *Nature*. Our whole benefits package, courtesy of Mother Earth, was valued at somewhere around 17 *trillion* dollars. Every year I see figures documenting how much birding, sport fishing, hiking, canoeing, and other recreational activities—and by extrapolation the wild regions in which these activities take place—are worth to local economies. These figures do benefit conservation, and I am grateful for them. But it shouldn't have to be that way. A place, a species, should be held most valuable for what it is—nothing more, nothing less.

~ ~ ~

Not everyone wanted a Goethe State Forest. I learned this combing through files of newspaper clippings, letters, and memos in the double-wide trailer that serves as forest headquarters. The proposed purchase of nearly 44,000 acres by the state from ninety-six-year-old lumberman J. T. Goethe in 1992 was in fact a matter of some contention.

In 1992, the Levy County Forest-Sandhills, as Goethe State Forest was known under its Conservation and Recreation Lands (CARL) designation, was considered the largest privately owned tract of old-growth pine remaining in Florida. It was thought to contain the most extensive unbroken expanse of longleaf pine flatwoods in the state. Conservationists deemed the property "a masterpiece of ecology" because of its undisturbed nature, diversity of ecosystems, capacious size, and undeniable attraction to no fewer than sixteen threatened or endangered species—the "best and largest contiguous habitat" for protecting the globally endangered Sherman's fox squirrel, said a spokesperson for The Nature Conservancy. The state agreed to pay Goethe and representatives of his deceased brother $64 million using funds from its Preservation 2000 program, money raised through the sale of bonds each year to buy endangered lands for conservation. It was more money than had ever been spent on a CARL project, but then the Levy County Forest-Sandhills were unlike any other land for sale in Florida. The citizens of Florida could not afford to miss this opportunity to save a unique relic of their natural heritage.

Opponents to the state purchase valued Goethe's land for reasons that had nothing to do with rare wildlife and "contiguous habitat." Levy County commissioners decried the loss of yearly tax revenues from the property. J. T. Goethe's land amounted to 6 percent of the county's total area. His 1992 property tax bill totaled about $130,000. As one commissioner put it, "a person should be able to do what they want to do with their property, but this sale would take much needed revenue from the county." This despite state law that would require 15 percent of revenues from forest timber sales be paid to the Levy County School Board, money for the county's children that would not exist without the sale. He also proffered his opinion as to the sensitive nature of the property, declaring that the forest was not endangered, but "good usable land."

Commercial timber interests worried aloud that ecosystem protection would prevent future cutting in the forest, although J. T. Goethe had not cut timber, with the exception of an area that had burned in 1981, on his property for more than fifty years. Many local folks were uneasy about the state's controlling so much land in the county. It smelled of a "land grab," as one writer stated in a letter to the editor of the *Gainesville Sun*. An anonymous ad ran in local papers:

$175,000,000.00

This is the amount of money the State of Florida Department of Natural Resources has to spend on special interest real estate purchases. This money is needed badly in the General Revenue Fund.

The public school system can't afford adequate facilities or enough teachers; the State can hardly meet its payroll, no pay raises are in sight and current ones are canceled.

The State of Florida is proposing to buy 54,544 acres of pure timberland in Levy County, Florida. This will take $16 million off the Levy County tax rolls. *You* will make up the difference.

If you are opposed to DNR's proposed purchase of the *unendangered* Levy County timberland, call your State legislators and local Levy County Commissioners and stop the Levy County Forest-Sandhills project.

I found a copy of the ad stuffed in the file with the other clippings. I was not able to find out who placed it.

Despite the hue and cry over lost tax revenues and state-sponsored land grabs to benefit "special interests"—that is, Florida's citizens—the land was purchased. Goethe State Forest is now open to the public for hiking, biking, hunting, fishing, wildlife observation, and uncontained tree hugging.

~ ~ ~

One morning in late August, I travel to the forest for a short hike. Near Goethe's western boundary, I turn onto Cow Creek Road, a narrow, two-track dirt path through the woods, drive a few miles, and then get out to walk. The air is thick and wet, customary for this time of year in north-central Florida. Overhead, in the pastel dawn sky, swirls of robin-egg blue infuse clouds as soft and gray as a mockingbird's breast. Thunder mutters sullenly in the distance. The drumming of woodpeckers echoes in the still air.

Fifty yards in front of me, a doe steps onto the road and pauses. We gaze intently at one another for several moments. Then she drifts off the road and vanishes into the brush as suddenly and quietly as she appeared. Sunlight shoots through thunderclouds to the east and the forest warms, the glow climbing the trunks of the pines to blaze fiercely in their crowns.

I glance skyward out of habit, in part to track the progress of the clouds and also to check for raptors. For most of the summer my eyes have been keened to the blade-like silhouettes of swallow-tailed kites. I know that by now the kites have begun their trek back toward South America where they winter, but my summer habit remains. In May, I had been invited by John Arnett and Audrey Washburn, assistants to Dr. Ken Meyer, an international authority on swallow-tailed kite ecology and migration, to join them and Division of Forestry biologists on a trip to check nests in Goethe. The kites typically build their nests in the crowns of tall, sturdy pines. We visited one nest in a stand of pines mixed with cypress. With a little coaching by Audrey and John, I was finally able to pick it out against the dim, overcast sky—a smudge of green lichens, small sticks, and drooping Spanish moss wedged in a fork of branches, nearly obscured by clots of needles near the top of the tree. By moving around to get different angles of view, we were able to distinguish the incubating kite's slender forked tail and wing tips protruding from the side of the nest.

Later that day in a clearcut, John and I watched a kite struggle against the wind with a branch weighted down by a long, thick strand of Spanish moss. The bird flapped vigorously, trying to gain enough altitude to soar, the moss whipping behind. We raced down the trail, trying to keep the kite in sight, finally losing it when a grove of young, twenty-foot-high pines blocked our path. Not more than ten minutes later, as we walked toward a stand of pines where we thought the bird might have landed, five more kites wheeled from behind the treetops, dipped low and then spiraled quickly upward in tight circles, borne on a great current of air, headed north. By now, the wind had shredded the overcast, and the sun shone brightly as islands of cumulus scudded west. The kites soared higher, their white bodies and black wings etched in sharp relief against the changeling sky. I watched until finally they vanished in the sun.

I have been looking for kites every day since then.

A dense mix of spindly longleaf pines and hardwood shrubs borders both sides of Cow Creek Road. Some of the longleafs are broader, taller, older than others. Many trees wear blue blazes, indicating they have been selected for cutting. I am saddened by this, although I realize the vegetation here is dense, the trees are too close together, and there is no regeneration of pines in the thick tangle of green life on the forest floor. And although I inherently distrust the Division of Forestry, perhaps because state politics pressure them to generate revenue from forests without adequate regard of environmental cost, Goethe's foresters and biologists have patiently explained their plans and shown me what they have already accomplished. Let me briefly recount what I have learned.

The Division of Forestry's Forest Resource Management Plan states the land is designated "multiple use," with "primary emphasis on the restoration and maintenance of native ecosystems, especially the longleaf pine ecosystem." According to Goethe biologist Carol Wooley, their restoration strategy does include logging—occasionally clearcutting planted stands of slash pine that will be replaced by longleaf, but most often selectively removing slash pines from areas where they mingle with longleaf, allowing the longleaf to re-seed the cuts naturally.

An area targeted for logging is first burned, then cut, and then burned again. The burning helps prepare the site for longleaf seedlings and encourages the return of native pinewoods understory plants. Nearly all areas of pine will be burned periodically, many during the summer growing season, to replicate the rejuvenating ground fires that once crept across the landscape. Old flat-topped pines and catfaces (trees scarred by turpentining) are spared from cutting and protected from burning because they are potential homes for red-cockaded woodpeckers, perhaps the most endangered of Goethe's wildlife and I imagine one of the more important initial reasons for the state's purchase of the forest.

Wooley spends much of her time studying the woodpeckers—checking nests, identifying active cavities (those cavities the birds regularly use), monitoring the health of the trees they are using, and keeping track of the number of birds. She says right now the forest supports two isolated populations totaling twenty-four clusters, or family groups, of two to five birds each. A mated pair relies on helpers—typically volunteers from previous broods—to help raise new chicks, much like Florida scrub jays and acorn woodpeckers in the western United States.

In spite of this intriguing survival strategy, the population of red-cockaded woodpeckers in Goethe and elsewhere is precarious. These woodpeckers carve their cavities into living pines, nearly always old trees infected with red heart fungus, which makes the wood softer and easier to excavate. But there is not enough mature pinewoods habitat remaining to support them. Population biologists say five hundred red-cockaded woodpeckers are needed to ensure a stable population in any given area. Each family unit requires two hundred to three hundred acres of old pine forest. Wooley thinks that only 33,000 acres of Goethe's 44,000 acres are suitable for the woodpeckers—not nearly enough for five hundred birds. And there is another problem looming on the forest's southern horizon—the planned expansion of the Florida turnpike—which could affect how the forest would be burned and, ultimately, the quality and quantity of habitat for red-cockaded woodpeckers and other pinewoods denizens near the road.

The turnpike currently reaches from Florida City, barely twenty miles north of Key Largo, to Wildwood in central Florida. The Florida Department of Transportation wants a forty-nine-mile extension linking Wildwood with U.S. 19 at Lebanon Station because "the upgrading and expansion of existing routes will still not meet the projected needs within this area of the state." The road will provide "a vital link in the state's plan for emergency preparedness" and "high speed access to points north of Orlando." This I learned from the note and accompanying newsletters mailed in response to my request for information from the Turnpike Authority in Tallahassee. In effect, the extension will funnel thousands of cars a day (at high speed) through what are some of the least developed areas in Florida, spawning gas stations, fast food restaurants, and motels (heaven forbid outlet malls) around four planned interchanges. Where new roads go, rapid development is sure to follow, altering the landscape and way of life of rural people here.

I doubt that building new roads to accommodate Florida's burgeoning human population will solve anything in the long term. Instead, we should be thinking and spending money on innovative ways to move lots of people using the transportation networks we already have. Perhaps more importantly, we need to think hard about how many people Florida can realistically support. This above all else should dictate "projected needs."

The Department of Transportation's original intent was to run the four-lane extension through the southern end of Goethe, effectively severing nearly 9,000 acres from the rest of the forest. Cost was intrinsic in this decision because the state already owned the land and it would be cheaper to develop than to buy private property. Several state agencies, including the Division of Forestry, Department of Environmental Protection, and the Florida Game and Fresh

Water Fish Commission, bitterly opposed the plan because it would, among other things, significantly restrict prescribed burning in the area due to the threat of heavy smoke on the roadway, destroy red-cockaded woodpecker habitat, disrupt the hydrology in nearby wetlands, and seriously impede the movement of wildlife through the forest, even with the promise of underpasses and fencing. The governor's office finally appointed a mediator to preside over meetings with the agencies to hammer out an alignment for the road that everyone could agree on. As I write, the exact placement of the road is still uncertain, although it will now entirely miss Goethe, instead falling somewhere between the forest's southern boundary and the Withlacoochee River. Once the alignment is determined, an Environmental Impact Report will be prepared and subjected to review and public comment.

Regardless of where the turnpike passes, its proximity to Goethe will make it more difficult for the Division of Forestry to buy surrounding land to increase woodpecker habitat in the forest. Large mammals, such as black bear, would have to contend with the road in their travels between the forest and wild areas to the south. Foresters could burn certain areas of Goethe only when they were sure no smoke would drift over the highway. And people like me, who appreciate their wilderness experiences free from the sounds of internal combustion engines, will most likely be forced to endure the unrelenting whine of traffic in the distance.

Thunder is louder now, closer, more insistent. The high, broad, cottony summit of the approaching storm has turned dark and ominous. A light rain begins to fall. Suddenly, the storm is on top of me. Gusts of wind tear through the close ranks of pines, showering Cow Creek Road with small branches and pine needles. But the sun is still shining, and the dense green world around me looks as if it is brushed with copper. Then, the light winks out, and it begins to rain in earnest. Thunder cracks. I run for my truck.

I am hard pressed to convey what Goethe State Forest means to me, at least concisely. My feelings dribble out through my photographs, as entries in my journal, in this essay. Alone, they are not particularly notable. But I have to wonder what would happen if every person in Florida took a moment to reflect on their favorite wild place, scribbled an address on an envelope, licked a stamp, and sent a picture, a poem, a letter, a leaf—anything at all—to the governor. Or to a senator or representative or anyone with the power to make decisions about wilderness in Florida. Just to let them know how they feel.

The flow of envelopes might be imperceptible at first, a trickle at best. But over days and weeks, it would increase, individual freshets of envelopes braiding into small creeks, tumbling toward larger streams, until finally they would meld into broad, swollen rivers, like the Suwannee or Apalachicola at flood stage, indomitable torrents of public expression advancing toward Tallahassee and Washington.

Imagine how sweet the scent of a pinewoods at dawn would be then.

Borderland

JANISSE RAY

I come upon the longleaf forest from the north, from my home in south Georgia, crossing the state line at Jennings. From any direction, I know, the landscape won't be much different—rural, agricultural, silvicultural. Not much rest for land in north Florida. Nor anywhere, I guess.

Cotton field. Pine plantation. House. House. Cotton field. Clearcut. Pine plantation. Field. Clearcut. Church. Trailer. Field. I see this everywhere I go.

After I cross the state line I pull over for a roadkill raccoon. I want to make Silas a coonskin cap and I need the tail; where the coon is killed a hawk's dead too, hit on the road, and I move both of them to the grassy ditch and saw off the coon's tail. It's large and bushy, striped, pretty. I feel odd, taking the tail like that and dumping the young coon unceremoniously by the road.

Where I-75 crosses the county road I stop at a convenience store. I forgot to bring mayonnaise for sandwiches. The store's full of smoke, and I know not to buy a box of crackers—brushing away a coat of dust to see the price—but I do.

More fields, more young pines. A few houses. Then, when I get to Blue Springs, where County Road 143 meets State Road 6, there's forest.

Longleaf forest.

It stands out like a skyscraper in a refugee camp, suddenly tall and very green, waving at the unremitting sky. Something in the back of my mind—some old, mossy, creaky memory of what a forest looks like—and I mean the forest that used to be here, that covered this land—gets triggered. It comes edging out, this old memory, as if I've been suffering from amnesia most of my life and just got hit on the head.

You'd have to drive a hundred, two hundred miles to see anything like this.

The damn forest looks so natural it's odd. And I get scared, thinking, *We have so little left we're forgetting what it looked like.* I have pictures of it in books at home and on my walls and in my files and in my mind. I've seen a couple virgin tracts, and some mature ones. Still I forget. What about people who don't know how it was—young people and newcomers and old people with bad memory? Heck, some grown people have never seen a real longleaf forest.

They may not like it at first. It takes some getting used to because there's only one kind of tree. Some people want more tree diversity than that—they want to be able to walk through a forest and say *magnolia, maple, hornbeam, cherry laurel.* I'd send those people about a mile west to the Withlacoochee River and have them meander in the floodplain.

But here, in the uplands, this is the way it's supposed to look. Just one kind of tree—longleaf pine—everywhere you turn. I like that.

Sometimes I want diversity—I don't want to wear blue every day, for example—but with these pines, I want stability. I want them relentless in their monotony, their monarchy. It must be a powerful tree that can claim a whole landscape for itself, a piece of a continent, from Virginia through the southern coastal plains, clear out to east Texas, 93 million acres. It has to be a noble, indomitable tree.

I'm meeting a man here. I don't know him well, but his name's Bane and he's from the same distance south in Florida. We met at a weekend dance a month ago and I liked him then—we liked each other. This place is midway between us, and midway is a good place to meet a man you don't know well, when you're single and sifting through men, hoping to find one who might come to mean what these pines mean.

It's a test. If he doesn't like the forest . . . I'll be more honest. A man I loved killed himself two months ago. A woman Bane loved died in an accident ten months ago, when a drunk driver slammed into six cyclists and killed the back two. Marta's death devastated Bane. Michael's devastated me.

Good thing the forest is intact, or close, its trees not virgin but mature, most about seventy-five years old. They are vigorous and healthy, and the forest appears to have kept all its pieces. I couldn't survive more devastation.

Bane is not yet at the meeting place, where the roads join in a flurry of litter. I park and walk out into the forest, eating cheese and crackers (they are stale), waiting. The woods have burned recently and my pants soon are streaked with black. I sit on a pine log, eyeing an empty gopher tortoise shell. I know Bane will come but maybe he's confused over roads.

I get in the truck and find him a mile away, picking wildflowers. "There aren't many," he says, grinning. He's prettier than I remembered, in his red flannel shirt and gold chain. I don't know how to act. So many changes lately, Mike's death, the move back to my devastated birthplace, a deep loneliness, a chasing after art and beauty in a diminished land.

The forester meeting us arrives. He works with the state Division of Forestry, the lead management agency for this tract—almost 2,000 acres—purchased in 1994 with CARL funds. Previously it was owned by Champion International and managed intensively as a quail-hunting preserve for the timber company's executives and guests. Two hired hands worked full time on the preserve, pen-raising thousands of quail and keeping the wild ones fed.

"This was their playground," Doug says. He is the forester. He looks like Dustin Hoffman, for real. He's clean-shaven, with chocolate eyes and dark eyebrows; his black hair throws gray sparkles in new sunshine. It's been raining for two days and we're camping tonight, so we're happy to see the sun.

Dustin Hoffman drives us around the old hunting roads. He answers any questions, but he's not verbose. The trees are fifty to ninety-five years old. The foresters burn about six hundred acres a year. Longleaf restoration is underway in the few fields on the property. He saw a bobcat here once. He doesn't know the names of the plants. There are red-cockaded woodpecker cavity trees, but they may be abandoned because the birds haven't been seen since 1994. One tree looks active.

It's not until Dustin Hoffman shows us where to camp and tells us the gate combination, just before he leaves, that I begin to see inside him. He tells me how he feels about his job, caring for the state forests in the area. "You're excited about staying out here," he says. "It's kind of like that every day, for me. Work is something I look forward to."

"You're a lucky man," I say.

"I know," he says. "On every desk that's made there should be carved a skull and crossbones."

Longleaf can't be talked about as a tree, really, but as the intricate and intriguing ecosystem that it is. You can't talk longleaf without talking gopher tortoise, nor tortoise without indigo snake, nor the snake without gopher frog, nor the frog without Bachman's sparrow. It goes on and on. There's a lot of talking to do.

All kinds of species are tied to longleaf pine and depend on it for their existence, and longleaf is tied to fire, depends on it, so all these species are tied to fire, and longleaf pine is tied to the highly diverse understory—all the grasses and forbs, like wiregrass and Curtiss' dropseed and showy orchis and blazing star—which is also tied to fire. The animals are tied to the understory.

Everything is tied together. All of us.

Bane's not an artist—never finished college—works for the power company. We don't have these deep-deep, center-of-the-earth, black-of-the-night conversations. But he's a good man. He knows how to love and how to cry. He's not scared. His eyes are kind.

We walk for hours, miles, in the forest, and he is not bored. He stays curious, engaged, kind. I discover that he likes nature, simplicity, frugality—good things to love in the twenty-first century—and I'm glad.

It is so good to be touched, loved in the way of skin and air, a whole night that close, the sky sagging with stars. I lie warm under the covers, this man I trust but do not know sleeping beside me, and think about the forest, how fragmented it is. In this one piece— almost 2,000 acres—it can be what it is supposed to be. It can function, can have what it needs, while all around, radiating from it, clearcuts and pine plantations and fields.

How desperately lonely I have been in the fragmentation, hanging on to remnants of beauty, spirit, art, touch, truth—them not growing around me but remembered. I have been fragmented in my homeland, these coastal plains, separated from friends, missing music and movies and art shows, cut off from much of what I know myself to be, waiting for the chance to flourish, to grow again. Waiting for the logging to stop and the land to heal.

Art Stockel, a biologist with the Fish and Game Commission, tells me that the gopher tortoises have been dying. Last year, after they burned, he found between twenty and thirty shells, glaring white against the scorched ground. "They were in different stages of decomposition," he said. "They didn't die in one year's time."

Across the highway, at Twin Rivers Wildlife Management Area, the loss is worse. "You could quickly count fifty shells," Stockel said.

Joan Diemer Berish, renowned tortoise researcher, tested live animals on the sites for the respiratory virus they can carry. The tests came back negative.

Then why are the tortoises dying?

Why did Mike die? Or Marta?

I worry about the animals. Certainly they become as much shells as I have been, at least in spirit, in the face of the fragmentation of a landscape they depend on. Surely the birds, who can cast an eye downward and see it all, know their loss. Undoubtedly they are as affected (we don't have to be saddened) as this fragmentation of spirit affects me.

If we call the things I have been missing poetry (what else is magic and spirit and truth?) then we can say I have been cut off from the landscape of poetry.

But this night, in this functional longleaf forest—where a young owl makes her harrowing cry in the dark silence and where deer tracks sprinkle the ground, where a juvenile raccoon scrambles up a sapling and peers around at us, where by day we spot almost every species of woodpecker possible—I am cradled in poetry. I can function, have what I need, be what I am.

On Saturday afternoon, with Bane napping, I again lie awake in the tent, loving the warmth, the quiet, the stillness, my drowsiness;

2,000 acres completely to ourselves; wondering again why it has been so long since I've felt whole. Then Mike. He is never far away but suddenly he is big, surrounding me, his face in front of mine: I miss him so much. I lie there crying quietly, trying to keep the grief at bay, thinking, *it gets me nowhere,* but Bane wakes up. "Why are you crying?" I know he will understand whatever I say.

Sometimes I felt Mike and I shared one spirit. I thought we'd have the long years of our lives to be friends. He just got tired and gave up. There is no place I can go where he is not dead.

Most of the longleaf trees in the Blue Springs forest aren't quite old-growth—their crowns haven't begun to flatten, nor have they gone to heart-pine. But they are close, closer than anything for hundreds of miles. It won't be long now.

The only thing I'm worried about is that it became a state forest, managed by Forestry. They're doing a good job with burning, and the land can tolerate the bit of winter quail hunting they allow. Doug said he doubted any timbering would ever happen, but I want to know for sure that's true. And I don't want to see a nature center built there.

I like it just the way it is, a forest suddenly springing from the fields, plantations, and clearcuts. I want it left alone to be as whole as it can be; that's more than enough. It's a place to heal the spirit. I want it for the long years of my life.

Brooker Creek

JEFF KLINKENBERG

Hunkered in the sand, I stop to admire the first coyote tracks I have ever seen close. "There seem to be more of them during the last few years," says Craig Huegel, manager of a place called Brooker Creek Preserve. I find it exciting that coyotes have come to my home ground, Pinellas.

Brooker Creek is not the Everglades, nor the Big Cypress, nor the Fakahatchee Strand. It is the wildest place those of us who live in Florida's most urban county have. It has lovely piney woods, shady oak hammocks, magnificent cypress swamps and wild, wild animals. What I like most about it is the delicious possibility of leaving a trail, hiking into the trees, and getting lost.

~ ~ ~

Brooker Creek lies east of Tarpon Springs, where Pinellas, Hillsborough, and Pasco counties come together. Outside the 8,000-acre county-owned preserve, progress is running wild. Bulldozers push over trees, cranes dig up the earth, and paving machines make sure highways are smooth and wide. New shopping centers are sprouting along the road like wire grass.

We all know progress is inevitable and, to a degree, welcome. Yet as our world gets more civilized, uncivilized places become even more valuable, especially to those of us destined to live in asphalt jungles.

"We need the tonic of wildness," Thoreau wrote in *Walden*, "... to wade sometimes in marshes where the bittern and the meadow-hen lurk, and hear the booming of the snipe, to smell the whispering sedge where only some wilder and more solitary fowl builds her nest, and the mink crawls with its belly close to the ground."

Craig Huegel—his last name rhymes, appropriately, with "eagle" —leads today's expedition accompanied by his friend LaVonne Ries, a volunteer at the preserve. We arrive in Huegel's four-wheel drive vehicle, and when the sand gets deep we walk. Now we hike in the belly of the forest, among the dwarf oaks and the stately pines and tall grass that threatens to devour the modest trail.

I can hardly believe I'm in a county where 3,000 people live per square mile, where traffic tends to be rush-hour bumper to bumper, where boom boxes thump night and day. Our soundtrack is provided by the chattering of gray squirrels and the twittering of rufous-sided towhees.

"I hadn't worked here long when I heard this strange sound," Huegel says, as we walk along. "The sound was coming toward me. I couldn't figure it out. It was the wind coming through the trees. The wind! I knew I'd been living in town too long."

~ ~ ~

I shudder when I realize how Brooker Creek, considered a prime development area, could have been lost forever. It is easy to shut my eyes and imagine the forest mostly gone and filled with pricey houses, golf courses, and neighborhood shopping centers, the street-lights shining on roads that cover earth where panthers once left tracks.

County residents voted to charge themselves an extra penny of sales tax. The so-called Penny-for-Pinellas helped buy Brooker. Lately the state also has spent tax dollars to add to preserve acreage, through Preservation 2000. Perhaps one day the panthers will ap-preciate it.

Years ago there were definitely panthers here, and there are people who claim that panthers still travel through the area. State wildlife biologists say Pinellas panthers are unlikely, yet from time to time credible witnesses say they have seen the large, tawny cats with long tails sprint out of the forest, cross the road, and vanish in the woods beyond.

In 1996, Huegel was walking on a preserve road when he discov-ered what he was sure was a panther track. He made a plaster cast and sent it to state panther experts. The experts said the track belonged to a large dog—a verdict Huegel still doubts. He earned his doctorate studying coyotes, and he knows dog tracks when he sees them.

"I don't think the preserve is large enough to have a panther popu-lation or even a bear population," he says, "but who knows? The preserve is surrounded by a lot of open land, and it's possible we could have some large mammals traveling through. I think there may be more panthers in Florida than people know about."

About coyotes there is no doubt. They invaded Florida long ago, and gradually they have worked their way south into Pinellas. Brooker Creek is the only place on which their presence has been documented. Welcome, coyotes.

"They will have an impact on wildlife," Huegel says, "but it's de-batable how much of an impact. Some people will disagree with me, but I don't see them becoming a problem, at least here. I'm hoping they'll fill a niche that wolves and panthers once filled—keeping the deer population at a healthy level. I'm hoping they will reduce the fawn crop every year."

Deer tracks dot the sand. So do the tracks of bobcats and foxes. I would love to see the wariest of large birds, the wild turkey. They're here, too.

"Here's a yellow butterwort," Huegel says, bending. We study the beautiful flower. It's a threatened species, but I'm even more excited by longleaf pines. At the turn of the century, they were Florida's dominant pine. Loggers took them first and replanted with faster-growing slash pines. Today, longleaf pines make up only 2 percent of our forests.

Animals that depend on longleafs for life—the red-cockaded woodpecker and the Sherman's fox squirrel—are threatened with extinction. No red-cockaded woodpeckers have been spotted in the preserve, but it is the best place in Pinellas to see fox squirrels. They're substantially bigger than grays, with long graceful tails.

~ ~ ~

On Saturday mornings, LaVonne Ries and other volunteers lead walking tours of the preserve by reservation only. Sometimes Ries walks slow and short distances, but sometimes, if her guests are fit, she walks long and hard. She is small and lithe and tough. For years she lived on an island that lacked running water and electricity. She feels at home in the preserve, although she carries a compass.

"I've been lost," she says, sounding exhilarated.

Everybody probably should be lost at least once in their life. I have felt lost three times in the Everglades.

Once the airboat on which I was riding broke down deep in the sawgrass at dusk. We knew where we were but knew we wouldn't be found without pushing the boat a long way to a canal. As night arrived, sawgrass cut my torso, and twice I stepped in water over my head, but you're reading these words, so you know my story has a happy ending.

I had another boating mishap in the mangrove section of Everglades National Park. Close to running out of gas, we decided to take a shortcut on the return to Flamingo. Hours later, we had no earthly idea where we were; all mangrove islands do look alike. Fortunately, the only boat we encountered the whole day belonged to a park ranger, who was happy to point the way to the main channel.

A few years ago I went on another wild boating adventure with an Everglades pioneer named Totch Brown. A former commercial fisher and alligator poacher, Totch wanted to show me his favorite old haunts. Some of the creeks were so narrow, and so overgrown, that we had to lie in the boat to pass. Totch was in his seventies and had endured three decades of heart disease. He had a graveyard cough. I clung to my compass.

"Where are we now?" I asked Totch all afternoon, getting him to show me on the charts. If Totch keeled over, could I get us back to Chokoloskee? I enjoyed my day with Totch, but I was relieved when my feet landed on the dock. The Everglades is the largest roadless area in the lower forty-eight states, and I am a city boy.

City boys need the tonic of wildness, and I seem to need it more than most. I don't want to get lost, really, but I like to walk right to the edge of it—just enough to be anxious.

~ ~ ~

Brooker Creek is not the most beautiful place in Florida, but it belongs to the people of Tampa Bay, and it is wonderful. With additional funding and management, one day it might be a state showpiece.

It is already close to that. Gopher tortoises sit at the mouths of their burrows watching us pass. A rare butterfly, the zebra swallowtail, lands on a paw-paw blossom. Ant lions, hidden at the bottom of little sand depressions, wait for something edible to tumble in.

We leave the trail. We're hiking cross-country now. Craig Huegel seems to know where he is going.

"I did get lost in here," he says. On his first hike, he guided leaders of Pinellas government right into the thigh-deep water of a cypress swamp.

Some people have all the luck.

The Wild Heart of Florida

SUSAN CERULEAN

Movement, height, and wind are the birthright of swallow-tailed kites, one of Florida's most breathtaking birds. The sway of treetops informs their bodies from the moment they are laid, curled in brown-splotched eggs. Seated in a rickety lawn chair on the forest floor, I am watching two of these birds—restless adolescent chicks with tawny breasts and heads—at their nest in central Florida's Highlands Hammock State Park. I am doing research for my book on kites and conservation in Florida, which requires equal parts watching birds and solitary musing.

The smaller bird crouches just inside the thick lip of the twiggy nest bowl, shifting its weight from foot to foot. Perched on a protruding branch two feet away, a second, heavier chick preens the transmitter harness fitted to its body just yesterday. The feathers of both birds riffle and rise at odd angles in the light gusty breeze. The larger bird extends its wings fully, then teeters in the wind, testing the properties of the element that will support it the rest of its life.

Earlier this morning, walking through the park campground on my way to visit this nest, I met a solitary walker, a gentle-faced man with nicely styled curly hair, a plaid shirt, walking stick. He scanned my fieldclothes and binoculars and sized me up as a proper person to receive his awe.

"This place is so abundant," he breathed. "It's almost too much!" And I remembered my first trip to Highlands Hammock, on a site visit for my first book, how, overwhelmed by the exceptional beauty of the virgin hardwoods and cypress, the throbbing, subtropical life of the place, I dubbed it in my own mind as "the heart of Florida."

But this time, I responded to the stranger, "Yes, and all of Florida used to be like this." A wet-blanket response to an open heart from a sore one. It has been hard to look at Florida this trip. Even the parks and protected lands seem worn. On the tiresome, eight-hour drive from Tallahassee yesterday, I saw plenty of bleak new development, but not a single swallow-tailed kite. In fact, between Ocala and Lake Placid on u.s. 27, I got the clear impression that the whole state was for sale, and to anyone's specifications, and real cheap. New subdivisions and mobile home parks sprouted along the state's spine of ancient sand dunes, offering seductive promises such as "permanent home quality at mobile home prices." The entrances to these places resemble used car lots, or carnivals, strung with plastic red, white, and blue pennants that snap and jump in the breeze. The individual flags are imprinted with enticing messages:

"Sale! Rock bottom prices!"

"Golf, golf, golf!"

"Welcome!"

Larger billboards describe the things for sale in more detail:

"Leisure Lakes Lifestyles Fore You!"

"Tropical Hardwood Estates: Manufactured Homes
from the $30s"

"Polo Park: Lakefront Retirement Living"

Mile after mile, Florida—and living in Florida—is offered up effort-
lessly, at the expense of whatever lived here before. And yet, every
one of us—sad, tired, desperate, poor, old, animal, human—deserves
a whole Florida, even if we don't know what it really is or once looked
like. Most of us, a staggering nine hundred new residents every day,
arrive eager to love our new place, just as I was eager to love Eckerd
College when I first moved to St. Petersburg from New Jersey in
1970. I never thought too hard about where my college was built—
on landfill over what used to be the productive mangrove coast of
Boca Ciega Bay. I didn't understand that the uniform ground cover
of painful sandspur meant the fill was so new and raw and sterile
that only the first line of colonizer—the sandspur—had thrown its
spiky seed and declared this new frontier its home. I never seriously
questioned the lack of life along the cement sea wall, never wondered
too hard why there wasn't an abundance of life there.

So much of Florida is built on the dead: the killed bays, the razed
scrub, the buried-alive gopher tortoise. We must deny these things
in order to live orderly, guilt-free lives. We remain ignorant. We
assume the best. We believe the cheerful corporate literature. We
delight in the descriptive names for our streets and malls and subdivisions: the Oaks Mall (trees cut down), Turkey Run (turkeys gone),
and so forth. We are guilty first of ignorance, second of strong self-
preservation instincts, third of laziness, and for some of us, that adds
up to evil intent.

Because we have not balanced growth and development with the carrying capacity and unique character of Florida, our public lands are increasingly pressed, loaded with the burden of being all we have of nature. It is as if I were to say, "The skin on my arms alone must perform all the functions my entire body's skin once did." All feeling must come through my arms, all sensation, all caress, all oxygen exchange, all function of skin. Only here can the sunshine touch me, or the wind.

Do we truly, thinking well, expect the preserved lands, those we somehow set aside, to perform all the functions of purifying air and water, stabilizing climate, providing home and nest space to all non-human forms of life? Don't we who purport to "own" land share in that responsibility? Why are we so careless with our true life support system and so completely fussy about our cars?

Actually, the awestruck stranger in Highlands Hammock resurrects in me some hope. He reminds me, despite my ungracious response, that each of us knows at a deep, instinctual level what truly connects us to life. And that Highlands Hammock and all the rest of natural Florida have a complex beauty that nothing we pave them with can ever equal.

An adult kite passes quickly through the branches above the nest, calling, "wheet, wheet, wheet, wheet, wheet, wheet. . . ." The chicks' response is imperceptible. The smaller one scratches its head. The other twists to preen its back, seeming to unhinge its tail at a ninety-degree angle in the process. Within days, these birds will master flight and not return to such a single-pointed existence until they sit on eggs of their own some years from now. They will mount the high thermals with hundreds of their kind, and the bright Florida sun will bleach the brown streaked feathers of their youth into pure white spirit.

The Ugliest Beach in Florida

JULIE HAUSERMAN

Don't bother making the trip to Topsail Hill. It's hot and buggy. The Panhandle is full of rednecks, no-see-ums, and tent revivals.

Go someplace civilized, like the Bahamas, where you can snorkel and collect conch. Go to Palm Beach, order a gin and tonic, and mingle. Surf Hawaii.

Just don't come here. And if you do, keep your mouth shut. I wish I did.

This used to be Florida's best-kept beach secret. People raved about nearby Grayton Beach State Park, considered one of the world's top ten beaches. They built a cute little town there called Seaside, then traded North Florida's traditional fried mullet and beer for gourmet food and fine wine. Yuppies and magazine writers arrived by the carful.

The magazine writers gushed about the stylish architecture, the sophisticated food, and the unspoiled beach. And I kept thinking: You ain't seen nothing yet.

Just down Highway 98, an unassuming, overgrown logging road led to the real paradise. It was Topsail Hill, a three-mile-long stretch of coast between Panama City and Fort Walton Beach. I used to nose my Toyota down that rutted road to find Florida's sandy soul. I had never seen such a wild Florida beach. Topsail's name was inspired by the spectacular forty-foot-high sugar-sand dunes, which are the state's tallest.

From out in the Gulf, the dunes look like a schooner's billowing sails. Behind them is a series of rare freshwater lakes, which move, geologically speaking, as the sea stakes its territory. The lakes are impossibly blue and full of bass.

As many times as I visited, I never saw another person there.

Stand on top of the dunes and you'll see what looks like low shrubs stretching from the beach to the lakes. But scramble down into the gully behind the dunes and discover that it isn't shrubs at all. It is a tiny forest.

The canopy of gnarled oaks is so low it brushes the top of your head. The ground is covered by pillowy, mint-green moss that seems perfect for a deer bed. From within this dwarf forest, you can look out at the lakes and hear the waves crashing on the other side of the dunes.

It smells like Florida ought to smell, salty and clean and blue.

I brought my young nieces here, and we pretended we were Indians, living between beach and lake, sleeping on moss beds and weaving vines to make a roof in the gnarled oaks. We walked inland, around the lakes, and found ourselves in a pine forest that gave way to a cypress bog. Beavers had built a house in the coffee-colored water, among the fantastic cypress knees.

"In 1937, Panama City Beach looked just like this property," said Carl Keen, a Panhandle park ranger who knows because his father still remembers.

It is a horrible thought. Panama City Beach is honky-tonk hell, with highrises and giant pastel dinosaurs. People flock there, to the Redneck Riviera, thinking they've found a summer paradise.

Just down the road, at Topsail, the sand tells stories. Walk in the dunescape early in the morning and you can read last night's news. Here, a raccoon's tracks clamber over a precipitous dune. There, a startled deer plunged its hooves deeply into the sand as it leapt into the palmetto. In another spot, a heron landed hard, leaving two deep depressions and then a trail of wispy tracks which vanish where the bird lifted its massive wings and took flight. Look closely and you may even see the tiny tracks of the rare Choctawhatchee beach mouse, an endangered species which vexes condo developers.

If not for that mouse, and America's savings-and-loan debacle, Topsail's dunes might have been bulldozed after all. As conservation victories go, it was a cliff-hanger.

For years, Topsail Hill was owned by one of Florida's biggest land-owners, St. Joseph Paper Company. St. Joe logged the inland pines, and left the beach and lakefront alone. Topsail was looking pretty valuable as the surrounding coast became more populated. But any potential developer faced an expensive fight over the endangered beach mouse.

Ultimately, though, it was the savings-and-loan crisis that saved Topsail.

In 1991, a newspaper editor asked me to check out a tip. In Walton County, a proposal surfaced to swap acreage in one popular state park—Grayton Beach—for acreage on privately held Topsail Hill.

When I opened the Department of Natural Resources file on Topsail, a bunch of news clippings fluttered to the floor. The stories were about savings-and-loan fraud in Texas, and they involved an undeveloped stretch of Florida beach. An alert reader in Texas had sent them to the state, and somebody had stuffed them into a folder and filed it away.

For the next several months, another reporter and I pored through mounds of papers and news leads that led us on a wild trail.

We found millions of dollars funneled to the Isle of Jersey, an offshore tax haven between Britain and France. We found a Panhandle developer with a $120,000 Lamborghini, a $153,000 gun collection, pure gold ingots worth $142,000, and $32,000 in loose diamonds. We found a lavish two-million-dollar Destin penthouse with 5,000 square feet of marble, Louis XIV antique candelabras, chinchilla throws, and velvet smoking jackets.

This opulence whirled around a grand scheme to develop Topsail Hill into the "Hilton Head of the Mid-South." It's questionable whether there were ever any real plans to develop it at all. In the end, two small savings and loan associations were dead, having lent millions on the phantom project, and taxpayers were on the hook for hundreds of millions to bail them out.

The crooks stole more than a hundred million dollars by puffing up Topsail's value, borrowing money, then running off with it. More than a dozen people were indicted, and the Federal Resolution Trust Corporation—the government agency that handled properties in the savings-and-loan crisis—ended up with much of the land.

Being alert to any gaps in the lockstep march to develop every inch of Florida's coast, conservationists acted quickly. Like Dudley Doright zipping in to save the maiden tied to the railroad tracks, The Nature Conservancy swept into Walton County and bought Topsail Hill from the Federal Resolution Trust Corporation at an auction on the steps of the Walton County courthouse.

Then, The Nature Conservancy sold it to the state through the Preservation 2000 land acquisition program. Topsail belongs to all of us now.

Before long, it will be a regular state park, with signs, rules, a real road, and a parking lot. My daughter Colleen, now ten weeks old, will be able to come here as an adult and see the beach the way I saw it.

I'm delirious to know that no bulldozers will ever carve into these steep dunes. But I'm churlish about sharing. To me, discovering a stretch of beach as wild as Topsail in modern Florida is as precious as finding a forgotten letter from a dead lover. As Joni Mitchell sang, "You don't know what you've got 'til it's gone."

Years ago, I interviewed David Brower, the iconoclastic founder of the Sierra Club. Before he became a famous conservationist, Brower was a mountaineer. For a time, he earned a living exploring California's most rugged country.

As a surveyor, Brower's job was to fill in the blank spaces on the map. He thought it was a wonderful and important vocation. But now, knowing what can happen to wild places, he wishes he'd never told anyone about those hidden valleys and secluded glens.

I took a boat trip with Brower and some other conservationists at Wakulla Springs, a state park outside Tallahassee. We glided across water as clear as an aquarium. We saw mammoth alligators on the banks, and herons in the trees.

Chatting with Brower, I boasted about North Florida's natural charms.

"There are gorgeous springs all over these woods," I blabbed. "I know one place where nobody goes, and there are about five springs there, clear as gin."

"Oh really?" Brower said, arching his eyebrow. "Where are they?"

Like a properly taught student, I paused, smiled knowingly, then shifted gears.

"It's way back in the woods," I said. "I couldn't begin to tell you how to get there."

Last of the Falling Tide

CARL HIAASEN

My father first took me to the Keys when I was six. He was a passionate deep-sea fisherman and had decided that I was old enough to join the hunt for blue marlin and sailfish.

The invitation was thrilling, but I had secret doubts about my suitability for big water. I suspected—correctly, it turned out—that I had not inherited my old man's cast-iron stomach.

But I wanted fiercely to experience the Keys. I'd wanted it since the day I'd seen an old photograph of my father, struggling to lift an amberjack that seemed nearly as tall as he was. The picture was taken in Key West around 1938, when my father was thirteen. He wore a white shirt and khaki pants, and with long tanned arms hoisted the fish for the camera. He looked as happy as I'd ever seen him.

Over the years, my father and grandfather told me so many stories that the Keys had become in my mind a mystical, Oz-like destination: a string of rough-cut jewels, trailing like a broken necklace from Florida's southernmost flank—the water, a dozen shades of blue and boiling with porpoises and gamefish; the infinite churning sky, streaked by pink spoonbills and gawky pelicans and elegant ospreys. This I had to see for myself.

On a summer morning we headed down U.S. 1, which was (and remains) the only road through the Keys. Although we lived in Fort Lauderdale, merely a hundred miles north, it might as well have been Minneapolis. The drive seemed to take forever. From the back seat I watched fruitlessly for evidence of paradise, but all I saw were trailer parks, gas pumps, bait shops, mom-and-pop diners, bleached-out motels, and palm-thatched tourist sheds that sold spray-painted conch shells. My restlessness took the form of whining, and from the front seat my father and grandfather instructed me to settle down and be patient. The farther south we go (they promised), the better it gets.

We passed the charter docks at Bud n' Mary's, where the great Ted Williams occasionally could be found, and suddenly blue water appeared on both sides of the Overseas Highway. To the distant east was the full seep of the Atlantic, deep indigo stirred to a light, lazy chop. To the near west was Florida Bay, glassy and shallow, with knots of lush green mangroves freckled with roosting white herons. At the time, I didn't know the names of these islands, but they were Shell Key, Lignum Vitae, the Petersons, the Twin Keys, the Gophers—places where I would spend, in coming years, hundreds upon hundreds of hours, none wasted.

The Keys never looked so enchanting as they did on that morning. As soon as we got to the motel, I grabbed a spinning rod from the car and made straight for the pier. Standing at the brim of those velvet horizons, gulping the sharp salty air, I understood what my father and grandfather meant. This was an honest-to-God wilderness, as pure and unspoiled and accessible as a boy could imagine. On my first trip to the Gulf Stream, I caught no marlin, only a bonito, but it pulled harder than anything I'd ever felt. It was a great day, made better by the fact that I'd managed to hold down my lunch.

The deep-running Atlantic was undeniably impressive, but the calm crystal flats of the backcountry intrigued me the most. To wade the banks was to enter a boundless natural aquarium: starfish, nurse sharks, eagle rays, barracuda, bonefish, permit, and tarpon, all swimming literally at your feet. The flats rippled with unique tidal energies—sweltering, primeval, seemingly indomitable.

This was around 1959, and nobody considered the possibility the shoals of the Keys might be destroyed, and that it might happen within a single human generation. Unimaginable! Life flourished everywhere in this tropical embrace, from the buttonwood hammocks to the coral reefs. The sun was so warm and constant, the waters so wide and clear, the currents so strong. Destroyed—how? By whom? Over centuries the Keys had survived droughts, floods, and the most ferocious of hurricanes. What was there to fear from man?

The worst, as it turned out. The population of Miami exploded during the next three decades, and urban blight metastasized straight down Highway 1, bringing crowds, crime, garbage, and big-city indifference to the Keys. The quaint and casual opportunism of the islands was replaced by an unrelenting hunger to dredge, subdivide, pave, build, and sell. It was tawdry, sad, and probably inevitable. By the 1980s, southeast Florida was home to four million souls, increasingly frenetic and determined to recreate at all costs. Where else would they go but the Keys?

I was one of them. A few years ago I bought a stilt house in a hammock near Islamorada. It's significant to note that Ted Williams, his timing still flawless, had already sold his place and fled Monroe County. The stampede of humanity was too much for him. My own friends gingerly questioned why a person would move to the Keys at a time when smart people were bailing out. Maybe there was a sentimental component to my decision—why, after all, does one sit with a dying relative? Duty? Guilt? Nostalgia? Maybe there was more.

Certainly I had no illusions about what was happening. As a journalist, I've written plenty about the rape of the Keys and the fast-buck mentality that incites it. On Big Pine, for instance, the federal government is doggedly buying up land to save the diminutive Key deer from extinction. Pro-growth factions have retaliated with lawsuits, high-powered lobbying, and old-fashioned venom. Road signs that alert motorists to deer crossings are routinely defaced—crosshairs painted over the emblem of a leaping buck.

As dispiriting as such cretinous behavior might be, the Keys also breed a devoted and tenacious species of environmentalist. About ten years ago, the hardwood forests and coral shores of North Key Largo were in danger of being bulldozed and dynamited into a series of huge condominium resorts. If completed, the developments would have brought as many as sixty thousand residents (and their speedboats) to a narrow belt of hammock situated between a national wildlife refuge and North America's only living barrier reef. You'd have been hard-pressed to find a more catastrophic location for a massive condo village. But local conservation groups banded together in opposition, and dragged slow-moving regulatory agencies into the battle. One by one, the seaside resort projects collapsed; today, much of North Key Largo has been purchased by the state for preservation.

That was a rare victory, but it made many of us believe that what was left of the Keys could be saved. To give up would be unthinkable, cowardly, immoral.

So I arrived to find the stores, tackle shops, restaurants, and highway jammed, even in the deadening heat of summer. This depressing state of affairs also applied to the bonefish flats and tarpon lanes. Raging and cursing, I've managed to cope; friendly fishing guides generously help me avoid congested waters, and I've marked a few hidden spots of my own. There are still plenty of fine fish to be caught.

Of course it's not the same place I knew as a boy. The best of it is gone forever. But if one knows where to look, and which tides to ride, it's still possible to be the only human in sight, to drift along crescent banks while schools of bottle-nosed dolphins roll and play ahead of your bow. These luminous moments become more rare with each tick of nature's clock. The Keys are in desperate trouble.

Not long ago I drove south past Bud n' Mary's and, on both sides of the Overseas Highway, the water was the color of bile—algae emptying from Florida Bay to the sea. A foul stain has settled around Shell Key, Lignum Vitae, the Petersons; on the falling tides it bleeds through the channels to the ocean. At the fishing docks, the talk is of little else. The old guides are sickened, the young ones are angry, and all of them are frightened for tomorrow. Wherever the cloud of algae appears, sea life vanishes. That which cannot flee dies. Already the baby lobsters have disappeared from Florida Bay, spelling future disaster for commercial crawfishermen.

Smaller blooms are not uncommon in the summer months, but the water ordinarily clears as soon as temperatures drop. Not in recent years. The chilliest days have failed to stop the spread of the milky green-brown crud. As I write this, about 450 square miles in the heart of the bay, Everglades National Park, is essentially dead. From the air, the sight is heartbreaking. If the algae continues to spill out to sea, it will smother the coral reefs, which require sunlight to survive.

For years, bureaucrats and politicians beholden to Big Agriculture have insisted that the "decline" of Florida Bay is unconnected to the egregious flood-control practices that have transfigured the lower Everglades. But this much dirty water was impossible to ignore. The algae bloom in Florida Bay became so vast and unsightly that tourists began to complain, prompting Florida's leaders to exhibit the first official signs of alarm. Assorted agencies, departments, and task forces are holding emergency sessions to discuss the crisis. A local congressman is asking that $3 million be set aside for more research. From Tallahassee to Key West, establishment voices are demanding swift action to replenish the bay, preferably before next winter's tourist season.

As if it was as easy as turning a spigot. It's not. Florida Bay historically was a brackish estuary, fed by a dependable, unimpeded flow of fresh water from the Everglades. As the state's population grew, the water from the glades was purloined and diverted through a network of deep man-made canals. This was done exclusively to benefit farmers, developers, and newborn cities, with no thought whatsoever to the profound long-term consequences. To this day, the golf courses of South Florida are more assiduously tended than the Everglades. Nature's plumbing has been rejiggered so that farms and cattle ranches can tap into the Everglades at will, use the water, then dump it back as waste. Florida's famous river of grass is being used not only as a fountain, but as a toilet.

The high-tech siphoning of the Everglades begins below Lake Okeechobee, at the sugarcane fields, and continues down to the tomato farms and avocado orchards of southern Dade County. The capture is so efficient that only 10 percent of the fresh water naturally destined for Florida Bay ever gets there. Many scientists believe this is why the bay is so sick. Without a seasonal flow from the East Everglades, the bay water has gotten saltier and saltier.

Several years of drought accelerated the transformation from estuary to hypersaline lagoon. By the mid-1980s, rich beds of turtle grass had begun to die and decompose, leaving bald patches on the bottom. The rotting grass became a nutrient for aquatic algae, which bloomed extravagantly in the salty, overheated pond. The algae, in turn, blocked so much sunlight that it killed the sponges and other marine organisms. The bay started turning to mud. Each year it looks worse.

Now it's early spring and the algae continues its spread. A steamy summer promises an eruption of new growth; airplane pilots and boat captains already report that bilious mile-wide puddles of the stuff have drifted out of the bay toward the pristine Gulf banks of the Lower Keys. Meanwhile, in the Upper Keys, floating clumps of dead sponges can be found from Flamingo to Long Key.

What can be done to save Florida Bay? Many experts say the most urgent priority is reviving the freshwater flow through Taylor Slough, which drains from the Everglades into the northeast part of the bay. A new trickle has been promised; getting more water will require taking it from Dade farmers and developers, who have powerful political allies in Tallahassee. And restoring flow is only part of the prescription—the water coming to the bay also must be free of phosphates and pesticides, and its arrival must be timed for the dry winter months. Too much fresh water can be just as lethal as too little, especially during the rainy season.

It doesn't take a marine biologist to know that tropical waters aren't supposed to look like bean soup, or smell like rotted mulch. These are not signs of a healthy ecosystem. Maybe the algae will die naturally, drowned by heavy summer rains, or blown out to the Gulf of Mexico by tropical storms. Yet even if we awake tomorrow and the stuff is gone, it's only a temporary reprieve. For the killer algae is but one symptom of many threats to the Florida Keys, each resulting from the uncontrolled invasion of man.

Runoff and sewage from high-density condos and hotels poison invisibly. Offshore, rusty freighters plow into the reef, while pleasure boats drag heavy anchors across the delicate corals. In the backcountry, manic water bikers and macho speedboaters frighten wading birds from their nests in the mangroves, disrupting centuries-old breeding patterns. Turtle grass beds—a crucial nursery of the marine life chain—are gouged, shorn, and crisscrossed by propeller ditches.

This is not what I want to show my son.

I first brought him here when he was a youngster, and I probably spent too much time telling him how splendid it used to be, before the greedy bastards ruined it. My boy listened but he also kept his eyes on the water—and fell in love with the place, prop scars and all. He got his first bonefish at age seven, and a big tarpon on a fly at age sixteen. He spends every spare moment here, including precious college vacations. On a recent spring morning when many of his classmates were slugging down Budweisers on the beach at Daytona, my kid was wading the flats of Long Key, scouting for tailing fish.

Battered, ragged, and long past their prime, the Keys continue to enchant and seduce. I can't blame my son for his weak heart, because there's still nothing as gorgeous as a calm dawn at Ninemile Bank, or a sunset in the Marquesas. The truth is, I always wanted him to love the Keys as much as I did, and as much as my father and grandfather before me. But if my son was to grow up fighting to save this place, he also needed to feel the sorrow and anger that come with watching something precious be destroyed.

He does feel these things, deeply, and that gives me a jolt of hope. The kid is damn angry about what's happening down here. Maybe angrier than his old man.

Where the Suwannee Meets the Sea

JEFF RIPPLE

March weather in northwest Florida is an unruly child, unpredictable and mischievous. One day might be breathless and warm and sunny, and the next morning a chill gale buffets the Gulf of Mexico, raising whitecaps and making travel by small boat—kayak in my case—miserable and sometimes dangerous. By evening, the wind may drop, and the Gulf becomes a perfect mirror reflecting the ebbing hues of the dying light. But I have learned never to count on this.

This morning I'm lucky as I launch my kayak from Shell Mound at the Lower Suwannee National Wildlife Refuge a few miles north of Cedar Key, drawing the last of an incoming tide, a balmy air temperature of 62°F, and a light but steady breeze out of the east. The morning sun is diffused by high overcast, and a low, dense bank of clouds crouches over the western horizon. White pelicans orbit a thermal, rising in slow circles as if climbing an invisible spiral staircase. Western sandpipers and ring-billed gulls watch with bright eyes from a mud flat as I paddle past, angling northwest on a course that will take me past Hog Island, Buck Island, and the Long Cabbage Keys before crossing the wide firth of Clark Creek to Deer Island, my first stop. From there, I'll aim for a long line of trees, hazy with distance, that marks where the wide, forked tongue of the Suwannee River finally tastes the sea. Two miles beyond that will find me riding the sinuous back of the river itself.

The Lower Suwannee National Wildlife Refuge claims twenty-six miles of a borderland to the Gulf of Mexico known by official state decree as the Nature Coast (formerly the Big Bend), where the peninsula of Florida arcs toward the north and west to join the Panhandle. It is a "low-energy" coastline, one where the wind rarely blows onshore with any consistency, as it does on the east coast and Panhandle, and so is characterized by salt marshes cleaved by numerous tidal creeks, shallow bays, a few coastal islands, and thousands of jagged, winding skeins of oyster bars. Mostly it is a vast estuary, a place where salt water from the Gulf mingles with fresh water from mainland swamps and rivers, including the Homosassa, Crystal, Withlacoochee, Waccasassa, and Steinhatchee rivers, as well as the broad Suwannee. Much is protected state or federal land within three national wildlife refuges and one state preserve.

After forty-five minutes of paddling, I approach Deer Island, having glimpsed a bald eagle soaring overhead while I was paddling across Clark Creek. A dolphin gave me a cursory inspection on its way out to the Gulf. Deer Island is one of several private—but completely undeveloped—islands within the refuge. About a mile long, it bristles with gnarled live oak, red cedar, cabbage palm, saw palmetto, and slash pine—typical of the coastal islands in this area. Its higher portions are connected by fecund swaths of low-lying salt marsh dominated by cordgrass and black needlerush. I beach my kayak and throw myself on the sandy shore. The tea-colored water is calm here in the lee of the island with the easterly breeze. The sun has become bright and hot, and I shed the spray pants I had pulled over shorts to keep my legs warm and slather on sun block instead.

Deer Island is remarkable for the long, crescent-shaped, white sand beach on its western edge, a feature many islands in this area lack. While some visitors may perceive the scarcity of good beaches in this region as a geological deficiency, I must admit I'm grateful. This circumstance alone has probably discouraged the building of wall-to-wall beachfront condos on the Nature Coast and slowed the onslaught of new coastal residents. The decided minority of folks who enjoy vast stretches of undeveloped hinterland, abundant wildlife, and quiet shorelines where encounters with their fellow humans are rare consider the area an undiscovered gem, a piece of relict "Old Florida." They are all too happy to direct beachgoers south to St. Petersburg or northwest to Panama City and Destin. I believe the residents of the Nature Coast, mostly commercial crabbers and aquaculturists, prefer it this way, too.

After a few leisurely stretches, I push off from Deer Island and paddle northwest toward a gap in the treeline on the horizon, which marks the mouth of East Pass. Once away from the lee of Deer Island, I raise my sail and skid over the chop until the wind slackens halfway across the bay, forcing me to drop the sail and paddle the remaining mile and a half to East Pass. To the west, I hear waves breaking on Halfmoon Reef, a long oyster shoal. The tide is falling.

In an estuary, tide dictates the movements of both humans and wildlife. Boating of any kind becomes increasingly difficult as the tide ebbs, exposing vast muddy flats that extend seaward from the marshes. On days when the wind howls from the northeast, even the scant few inches of water that normally lie at low tide in natural channels through the flats vanish. Fiddler crabs gather to feed en masse, sweeping over shorelines in such numbers that it is as if the land itself has picked up and clickity-clicked away. Flocks of shorebirds follow and gorge on this mobile smorgasbord. As water flows out of marshes into creeks that widen into bays, it sweeps many small animals toward the Gulf, where hungry mouths wait for them in eddies or deeper channels.

This process is reversed when the tide begins to rise and flood the oyster bars and salt marshes. Predators move in with the water to feed. From the kayak, on a high tide, I often watch stupendous fish moving through shallow water above oyster bars, their broad tails flapping the air. These are usually black drum and red fish (red drum), which frequently grow to more than fifty pounds. The fish love crabs, at times literally standing on their noses as they energetically search for the reclusive crustaceans among crevices and holes in an oyster bar. Sheepshead—flat, vertically striped, heavy-scaled fish that remotely resemble freshwater sunfish—also target crabs at high tide, ghosting along the edge of a bar in slightly deeper water to take advantage of the bold and the foolish.

Estuaries have been called the cradles of the sea because so many marine creatures spend their early lives there. Through these protected nurseries tidal water ebbs and advances—the sea's pulse, slow and rhythmic. To walk a mud flat as the tide boils around your feet is to shuffle through the pounding blood of the planet. On both tides, nutrients and organisms pass between the salt marsh and surrounding near-shore waters in an unrelenting cycle of nourishment and death.

The Suwannee meets the Gulf of Mexico like a snake with its mouth full. Born in the Okefenokee Swamp of southern Georgia, the river has distended and coiled its way through northern Florida for more than two hundred miles before gaping at the Gulf, grasping Hog Island (not the same Hog Island I passed near Shell Mound) in its maw. The river swirls around the island—shaped rather like a monstrous, tailless stingray—splintering into several passes, of which East Pass and Alligator Pass are the largest. Hog Island is a massive clot of river swamp, marsh, and brackish creeks that on my USGS map look like spider veins spreading across white paper flesh.

As I follow East Pass upstream, itself several hundred feet wide, Hog Island squats to my left. I paddle until Dan May Creek wriggles away to my right about a half mile from where East Pass empties into the Gulf and then dip a finger into the inky water and taste. No hint of salt. Even without sampling, I know I'm in fresh water by looking at the plant communities bordering the pass. Where at the mouth I had kayaked beside black needlerush and cordgrass— prominent salt marsh species—I now am flanked by sharp-toothed embankments of saw grass, a freshwater sedge, intermixed with needlerush at the shoreline.

Another half mile puts me past the marsh and into river swamp. This part of East Pass resembles the Suwannee of legend. Majestic bald cypress, tupelo, and red maple line the muddy bank. I spot in this stretch more ospreys and their nests in close proximity to one another than I have anywhere else along the coast. There are at least a dozen individual birds, possibly more that I don't see. Two have nests no more than fifty yards apart. The ospreys' ringing chirps echo between the forested banks of the pass and shadow me for the remaining distance to the river. Sturgeon roll, drawing the dark Suwannee over their backs like greatcoats, and less than a mile from the river, I watch two manatees frolic near shore, either mating or playing. The manatees disappear as a powerboat races too fast around a bend. Perhaps they know firsthand the impact of a boat hull or its slashing propeller. The whine of the engine drowns out the ospreys, and as the boat passes from sight around the next bend, its wake rolls under me and into the swamp, slapping noisily against tree trunks.

Even within a refuge, it's almost impossible to find measureless sanctuary. Nearly all federal lands—parks, wildlife refuges, forests, preserves, monuments—are mandated to accommodate a variety of personal and commercial human uses, some incredibly intrusive, including jet-skis, powerboats and airboats, snowmobiles, mining, logging, and military flyovers, that in my mind discourage attempts for more personal, spiritual explorations, such as hiking, canoeing, wildlife observation, or ethical hunting and fishing. Worse still, the welfare of the land and its wild inhabitants—the underlying reason for the purchase of federal conservation lands—is often compromised as a result.

Clouds obscure the sun again, and the western sky has darkened to the color of a manatee's skin. I'm running out of time. I reach the Suwannee, tie my kayak to a tupelo, and eat a late lunch among a nest of roots. The tapestry of cypress and tupelo, alligators and sturgeon, even the bright, hot fury of the ospreys dim in the gathering gloom. The Suwannee shoves its obsidian bulk through the trees, strong and fluid, toward the sea. I turn my kayak and flow with it, pointed home.

River of Dreams

JOE HUTTO

With the possible exception of light, nothing is so vital to the existence of life on earth as pure, liquid water. Similarly, and by no coincidence, these two fundamental entities appear also to be most significant in identifying and defining the realm of the human spirit. Light and water are the universal human icons, and across all cultures and all times seem to be the vehicle for, or the embodiment of, the mystical, the sacred, and the divine. Who could imagine a perfect place, an ideal world—a paradise—without the image of abundant, clear water—cascading crystal streams to stir the spirit, and deep, limpid pools, through which, and at once, we can envision both the depths of our own experience and see ourselves perfectly mirrored within the world. It is probably only by reflection that we may perceive our own membership in the universe.

Ironically, no greater potential for unpleasantness exists in all of nature than with those two most volatile and unstable of elements:

hydrogen and oxygen. One needs only recall the *Hindenburg* to be reminded of the inherently violent potential of this union. But, that this marriage arranged in chemical and physical Hell could conceive that most benign and life-giving of compounds, the antithesis, the antidote to combustion—H_2O, water—is a wonder that falls well within the realm of the miraculous.

Although hydrogen and oxygen are among the most abundant of all the elements in the universe, liquid water is in fact an extremely rare and unlikely substance. The universe as we know it is mostly empty space, and an ambient temperature for any given location in space might hover around minus 300°F. Exceptions to these norms occur suddenly, frequently, in the form of stars like our own sun—a diminutive example, but with temperatures exceeding 40,000,000°F.

Water in its liquid form can only persist within an extremely narrow 180°F window between ice and vapor. In a cosmic environment of such dramatic extremes, a persistent liquid water refuge is an overwhelming mathematical improbability. If chemical elements occur throughout the universe in similar proportions, and there is some evidence to suggest that this may be the case, then it is possible that even gold occurs in greater abundance within the cosmos than pure liquid water. Water must be identified not as mere chemistry but also as the extraordinary stuff of miracles, of legends, of dreams.

Florida, blessed by an unusual geology, may be one of North America's last great reserves of pristine, clear water. An underlying labyrinth of ancient limestone is gradually revealed as the Carolina Piedmont recedes toward the Gulf Coastal Plain. Rising from hundreds of feet below, sparkling waters that have secretly percolated and flowed southward for perhaps hundreds of miles emerge through various areas of the state. Vast quantities of crystal liquid surge upward and then, suddenly, through deep, indescribably blue chasms—hauntingly—as if welling up from the eye of an angel, a magnificent river is born. From these mysterious depths a perfect elemental substance rises, and if there exists any mystery and wonder in the human spirit, perhaps it too may be compelled to rise and be born there as well.

These rivers have always been magnets for a rich and varied fauna. The fossil bones of creatures that survive today mingle on sandy bottoms and in protected limestone pockets with those that died out tens of thousands of years ago—camel with deer, tapir with turtle, giant sloth with gator, mastodon with fish. Here lies a silent menagerie, a mute gravel of lost bones whose magnificent forms once bellowed, growled, and roared, echoing across these same clear channels, and, for those who want to hear, still reverberate across the river swamp like distant thunder.

Humans, like many other creatures, have always found spring-fed rivers to be places of opportunity. Strange names such as Homosassa, Weeki Wachee, Ichetucknee, Wakulla, and Wacissa—to name a few—reflect a rich Native American presence, people who for more than ten thousand years were irresistibly drawn to these rare environments. Florida's rivers have long known the murmur and laughter of the human voice. A ubiquitous but discreet litter is scattered uniformly along the banks and shorelines, and throughout the rivers' shallow runs and channels. From the glassy flint debris of the ancient wandering mammoth hunters to the more recent sedentary ceramic traditions, bits and pieces representing millennia upon millennia of human prehistory now silently lie with the shattered bones of great creatures now vanished. Abundant wildlife and plants have always drawn people to rivers for nourishment. But one needs only lay eyes on a sparkling, spring-fed river to realize that something else subtle and profound is offered here—a nourishment of spirit.

The specific physiography of the land through which a great spring rises gives each of its rivers a distinct ecology, an obvious look and feel; each, somehow, is recognizably unique. Because Florida's springs typically emerge along the karst coastal plain, they are characteristically short, and opportunities for accumulative degradation are thus lessened. The coastal plain is further characterized by low, poorly drained soils from which rise pine flatwoods and swamps. Often, Florida rivers are bordered by vast, primeval, old-growth river swamps—in some cases miles wide—that harbor cypress, sweet bay, tupelo, and sable palm, historically affording no practical access for roads and bridges, no high ground for development. With few notable exceptions, Florida's native rivers are not imperiled by industrial pollution as are rivers in other areas of the nation, but rather are in danger of simply being loved to death. The adoration, and in some cases greed, of otherwise well-meaning people has turned any Florida riverside exposed above mean high water into "waterfront property." It is a shocking and heartbreaking sight to round a bend on a seemingly wild river and suddenly see the world reduced to so many "lots," each trimmed to provide its "view," each with its boathouse, each with its dock providing access to dilapidated concrete bulkheads and eroding banks, each house with its septic tank and drain field lying only inches above solid rock. The nature of a river is not about ownership but rather about membership and fundamental relationship—geological, biological, and social—with the society of living things. A river is not merely the expedition of water from an origin to a destination but instead a complex, living, indivisible entity, and as in all life, exists as a product of its birthplace, its history, its integration with the land, and its nourishment. The bodily essence of a river is one of unimaginable power, but its wild heart and soul are fragile.

The Wacissa River in Jefferson County is one of Florida's best remaining examples of an unspoiled spring-fed riparian ecosystem. Geography has favored the Wacissa with nearly complete inaccessibility, insulated by a vast surrounding river swamp ranging from a mile wide to as much as three. This submerged river valley is in turn surrounded by great expanses of poorly drained pine flatwoods interspersed with a complicated mosaic of cypress heads and impenetrable titi swamp. Unlike most rivers, roads have never paralleled its course; only a grid of rough logging roads in the area now provide access for pine pulpwood harvest.

Originating from no fewer than twelve major springs and numerous smaller ones with names like Big, Garner, Blue, and Buzzard Log, the Wacissa flows unobstructed by roads, boat landings, or bridges for nearly fifteen miles to its confluence with the Aucilla River, several miles north of the Gulf of Mexico. Exceptions to this exist at Calico Hill, a small Pleistocene dune ridge that affords a little high ground and some privately owned land with a few structures, but no public access. The public gains access to the river only from the rise of the springs, a mile below the small community of Wacissa, or from a single landing at the lower end, known as Goose Pasture.

Below Goose Pasture the Wacissa loses its identity and becomes a complex maze of rivulets that join forces with Cow Creek and eventually merges with the black water of the Aucilla. A well-marked canoe trail now prevents the occasional boater from spending an unanticipated and probably unpleasant night in a north Florida wilderness. A side of Florida's dark past is revealed in the western-most run, known as the "old slave canal." Improved by slaves in the 1800s to provide cotton planters with more direct access to shipping, an otherwise beautiful natural environment becomes a silent monument to unthinkable misery and brutality.

Although the surrounding native pinelands have been decimated by clear-cutting and slash pine "plantation," the river swamps and drainages are largely intact and preserved. Perhaps nowhere else in Florida can so much contiguous wild river be observed. This is still bear country, where deer and wild turkey also abound. Birds of prey may be seen at every turn. The cries of ospreys and red-shouldered hawks resound through the canopies of aged cypress. Bald eagles soar and swallow-tailed kites float weightlessly by, dipping occasionally to retrieve some small prey from the highest branches. A black vulture pumps its powerful wings when roused from its sanctuary. Great, flashing pileated woodpeckers nest in old hollow snags, and the brilliant prothonotary warbler prospects for insects among the hazel alders. Wading birds thrive in these environs, with a rich diversity of native herons, ibises and wood storks, and in winter, many species of migrating waterfowl feed in the lush aquatic vegetation that flourishes in these clear, fast-moving waters. This vegetation in turn supports a rich population of ampularia, or "apple snails"—a favorite food of the limpkin. The rare, haunting call of the limpkin in some way helps to define and personify this river's singularly wild identity. Sadly, the echoing cry of this bird is the lost call of much of Florida's wilderness.

From the first iris of spring to the rich red cardinal flowers of summer and later the brilliant swamp sunflowers of autumn, a spectacular progression of color is unfolding to delight butterfly, hummingbird, and botanist alike. Big, black, rubbery alligators abound, as do other reptiles, including a noteworthy population of the endangered indigo snake. Brown and banded water snakes are visible here and there, and in quiet, protected shadows, the secretive cottonmouth awaits its prey. The Wacissa's mature cottonmouths retain strikingly vivid color patterns, testifying to the purity of the waters in which they live.

The Wacissa River is at once a place of community and of solitude, a teeming biological community where a person can share in the society of other living things and know that while in the company of wilderness, loneliness is never the companion of solitude. Such a wild spring-fed river is a rarity in all the world. It allows an increasingly uncommon opportunity for us to behold the world as it has always been—a single vision of the earth, intact and unchanged for perhaps thousands of years—a remnant primeval connection to our source. The human spirit is always in need of wild places, particularly wild rivers. Here we can thoughtfully observe our direct relationship to life, our own transitory nature, and be grounded in the knowledge that we are but the briefest of footnotes in an ancient and vastly greater design. It is the proper existential reality—one that can stir the imagination to dream and grace the human heart with wings.

A Valley of Inches

The Headwaters of the Upper St. Johns River

BILL BELLEVILLE

Along with 3.5 million others, I live in the St. Johns River "Valley" in east central Florida. For a person to reside in this sprawling 8,840-square-mile section of river basin is not particularly a rare or special event. To fully realize that you do, surely is.

Like much of the rest of natural Florida, this is a valley unique unto itself: There are no towering hillcrests, no mountainous slopes, no high-profile ravine walls.

Instead, it is an enormous sprawling sand and limestone basin gradually drained by the nearly imperceptible slope of its young terrain, a landscape that has repeatedly been carved and molded from the sea in recent geological time. It is a sculpting that continues today, with the dynamics of currents, tides, weather, ship traffic, and dredging all leaving slight but sure thumbprints on the malleable channel that marks the river's course.

From its headwaters to its confluence with the ocean, the river in this valley falls only twenty-seven feet—barely an inch a mile. If I lived atop more hardfast land and rock back on the mainland, this distinction of inches would be virtually lost to all but a few concerned with the measuring of topography by degrees.

But in Florida, where an average five feet worth of precipitation falls atop this region yearly, an inch means something. Here, the slightest depression in the terrain becomes a slough. Natural furrows are transformed into creeks. Broad, pancake-flat savannas brim with rain, birthing entire headwaters.

Because this is all done under cover of magnificent subtlety—inside a fretwork of wetland plants, spread over a massive basin, miles from dry land—this process can seem tedious, even cryptic. For those used to having the world neatly delivered to us in this turbo-charged age of immediate gratification, figuring out a river as complex as the St. Johns is like counting the number of angels on the head of a pin. For believers, it can be done, but it takes time.

Yet, the entire process of discovery can be entirely missed, unless you focus on the act of looking—not just where to look, but how. "Nature and books," as Emerson once observed, "belong to the eyes that can see them."

To fully see a river like the St. Johns, then, is an act accomplished by patience, a matter of degrees.

For me, this act of seeing the river begins in my own backyard.

The weathered cracker house I call home was built on a chunk of drained wetland almost a full mile from where the St. Johns dilates itself into Lake Monroe, about midway along its 310-mile meander to the sea. The resourceful farmer who once raised livestock and row crops here inside a perimeter of bamboo and sour root citrus trees—

his tinkering with twig grafts never fully complete—is gone now. And so are most like him, an entire community that once farmed celery and tomatoes and squash in the black, muck-rich soil where the wetlands used to be.

The hope that drew them all here, as well as the methodology that kept them, is still imprinted on the land. And so it is with my own land, down here at the end of a dirt road, next to the freeze-burned citrus grove, overgrown now with sabal palm and live oak and a thicket of blackberry vine, still guarded by the shrill cry of red-tailed hawks.

The boundaries of my yard, like those of my neighbors, are bracketed with ditches. Layered with grasses and ferns, they seem almost natural, except, of course, for their sheer linearity. They run east and west, and then, north to the river, precise and angular routes that efficiently expunge the wet from the wetlands. In turn, they offer expediency and rich, tillable soil in a Faustian trade that even a half-century ago probably seemed like a great deal.

Because most of Florida's population is new, we see only the grooves left behind in the earth. There is scant cultural memory of what was here before. Even on my little dirt road, which seems lifted out of a corner of Cross Creek, none of my contemporary neighbors can recall a landscape without ditches.

It takes an aged, faded survey map of the property to show a time when there were none. On that seventy-five-year-old map, there is only a light line meandering through what is now my back yard, intent on making its way to the St. Johns in the full spirit of whimsy God grants to tiny creeks.

This little stream with no name has only vanished in part. Its flow still lives, revitalized during the wet season, filling the narrow ditches with two and three feet of water and gambusia, fed by a larger earthen gutter on the far side of the dead grove. All of it is geometrical, ordered, like lines drawn by a diligent youngster on a giant Etch-a-Sketch. This is water management in its most simplistic form, a technique that has drained at least half the wetlands from our peninsula—including the basin of the St. Johns.

But there are more secrets here in the valley. In my front yard, I look closely at the edges of the clay road to see how its foundation is composed. Underpinning a road like this in a region as wet as Florida is not easy. Boulders and smaller igneous rocks like you might find in more ancient terrains are virtually absent. How could the road builders in the 1920s and 1930s build pavements they could be sure of?

The resource they often used was not geological, but cultural. I look closely at the hardpan and see it is comprised of millions of tiny, sun-bleached freshwater shells—gastropods and bivalves. They are shells that were once part of a midden heap—maybe even a burial or ceremonial mound—created by prehistoric Indians in the valley over thousands of years, an edifice rich in the hardness of calcium. For road builders with nowhere else to look, folks anxious on "reclaiming" this moist terrain, the mounds spelled cheap and abundant fill.

As a result, the dirt road to my house, then, is paved with the remnants of just such a mound, virtual pages of long-forgotten aboriginal history scattered from mailbox to mailbox, flattened more thoroughly with every crunch of our modern tires. On other such older roads throughout the basin, children sort through the fill rubble for arrow points and pieces of pottery.

And so my own little rustic tract of Floridiana graphically tells the larger story of how man has generally regarded the St. Johns and its cultural history, here in the deepest heart of the river valley.

The fact that a healthy river remains at all, that it is still magnificently wild in many parts, and that its banks are still dotted with ancient Indian mounds, is a testament not to man's restraint, but to just how pervasive and powerful this resource actually is.

If memory is the simplest form of prayer, as the poet Marge Percy once wrote, then we are perhaps losing our collective memory about the river, forsaking our right to exalt with this self-induced amnesia of its historic ecology. Examining the traces of my yard—indeed, any land inside the St. Johns River Valley—will set loose this history, providing clues of where the river has been.

To figure out where it might go, I have to travel down to the bottom, to the heart of its headwaters, where a broad, saturated marsh has the faintest dream of becoming a river.

~   ~   ~

A lone snail kite soars overhead like untethered origami, a white ibis pokes its half-bow of a beak into the mud, and the ghosts of long-gone ivory-billed woodpeckers worry the trees in the distant hammocks. Whales once breached here, somewhere above where I am now standing, thigh-deep in saw grass at the river's headwaters. They did so worldwide of course, back when they were something other than whales, and land was little more than the remnants of angry, fuming volcanic pinnacles. But age is the great divider, and geological time—or the lack of it—was, and still is, what has made Florida and its waters unique.

Florida is young, freshly washed from the ocean in a recurring series of Ice Age fluctuations that has reconfigured its soft coastline as sea-born escarpments.

During the last series of these reformations, when the appendage that would be Florida was as truncated as it appears on old Spanish maps, the terrain that would hold the St. Johns River Valley finally arose. This valley was born as a deep saltwater lagoon, bordered by a perforated line of sea islands and bars to the east, and by the ancient ridge to the west. The time was 100,000 years ago, and sea level was forty-two feet higher than it is today.

In this way, then, the basin that would one day cradle the St. Johns was not molded by the torturous chasm of shifting plate rocks or scooped out by tedious erosion through a steep ravine. Instead, it cascaded down from the sea in a timeless trickle of shell and sand and bone of animals and calciferous plants, marine life that once swam, crawled, and took root here. The walls of this valley were constructed of ancient dunes and terraces, shaped into north-south contours by the energy of the wind and the spindrift of the prevailing littoral currents offshore.

But the ocean that shaped the early basin of the river was not through yet. When the sea level dropped one last time, and the coast and dune line migrated even closer toward the Atlantic, the function of the marine lagoon moved with it, setting up shop inside the parallel basin of what would become the Indian River.

Left behind, bereft of its estuarine nature, the just slightly older inland valley did what many of Florida's brand new residents continue to do today. It re-created itself anew.

It did so with the abundance of rain onto the southern subtropic realm of this peninsula, an act that relies on the wealth of foliage and water to keep the cycle in good working order. The warm sun sucks moisture up into the cumulus, and the sky sends it back down again onto the great sprawling basin as drizzles and showers and great heaving bursts of thunderstorms.

And somewhere here, somewhere around me, west of Vero Beach and Fort Pierce, the alchemy of a river is fused from the over-saturation of water into the land, birthing a tenuous flow that slowly—if not always surely—heads north for the sea.

In the greatest of ironies, of the kind only a flat place like Florida can acknowledge, another giant river system parallels the St. Johns on this same latitude, not so far away. But instead of flowing north, it is busy moving south.

This other river system is inland from here, barely twenty miles away on the other side of the relic marine terrace of the seminal St. Johns valley. It is the Kissimmee, and the scant rise of Florida geology—an accident of nearly forgotten sea bottom history—moves it through its own basin, south to Okeechobee, for it is the origin of the grassy river of the Everglades, a place that—thanks to politics and media notoriety—has become considerably more seen than the St. Johns.

A Ribbon of Wilderness

The Savannas State Reserve

ANN MORROW

I leave the red clay hills of my north Florida home early in October and head south on U.S. 27, away from the Panhandle and onto the coastal plain of the peninsula. Near Chiefland, I cut east, toward the thoroughbred country of Ocala, crossing Florida's ancient sandy spine, the Florida Central Ridge. I'm on my way to the Savannas State Reserve near Fort Pierce on the East Coast. I'll find the Atlantic Coastal Ridge there, another Pleistocene sand dune, forming the eastern boundary of a chain of marshes and lakes. The two sandy ridges I'll encounter on this trip are strong reminders of tides that ebbed and flowed with the rhythm of the ice ages, sculpting this long sandbar of a state.

The ridges are oriented north-south, and so it seems is everything else. Roads, rivers, dunes, and islands conform to this geometry. A ring-billed gull flying inland to forage from the breaker line of

Hutchinson Island would pass, first, over the elongated barrier island and then cross the Indian River. Continuing its flight past the low coastal ridge, the gull would look down on the shallow waters of the Savannas, one of the last examples of coastal freshwater marsh in southeastern Florida, before passing the narrow strip of slash pine flatwoods that forms its western boundary. Beyond that, it would encounter a thick band of subdivisions and the commercial strip along U.S. 1 where, if it was lucky, the gull would successfully panhandle a meal or two.

The geologic forces that shaped these linear features are hard to ignore, but more than that, I am aware of the human ones that have snipped off the northern and southern ends of the Savannas and pressed in on it from both sides. The Savannas State Reserve is ten miles long and barely a mile wide in spots. Explorations here are not wilderness experiences requiring sophisticated gear and careful planning, although the heat and insects can be life-threatening.

In the late afternoon, I begin my reconnaissance of the reserve with my good friend Barbara, an old college roommate and native plant aficionado. A west Florida native, she is anxious to set foot (and paddle) in this unique east coast landscape. An onshore wind is blowing in a constant parade of clouds from the Atlantic as we head south on narrow, two-lane Indian River Drive. To our left, the embankment drops down to the brackish waters of the Indian River lagoon, where wooden docks reach out for deeper water. Across the river, we can see the cooling towers of the power plant protruding from the flat green line of the barrier island. On our right is a single band of houses, sitting on the slopes of the Atlantic Coastal Ridge. The Savannas lie just on the other side of this sandy hump. Ten thousand years ago, when Hutchinson Island was a mere offshore sandbar, high-energy waves thrashed against this ancient shoreline. The shallow freshwater basin that sustains the Savannas once resembled the Indian River we see today.

We turn onto a side road, and the car creeps up the old dune, now mostly paved and subdivided. At the top, we pull off near Gate 13, an inauspicious boundary marker and the start of the Savannas Hawk Bluff Trail. We get a magnificent sense of height and can look west over oaks and sand pines to the opposite side of the Savannas. Houses here strain for vistas in all directions; rooftops are capped with picturesque cupolas and widow-walks. One hundred years ago, we could have stood on this spot and looked out over a broad expanse of pineapple plantation, an industry that flourished on these ridges for about thirty years. The community of Jensen Beach to the south was briefly known as the pineapple capital of the world. As Barbara and I squeeze through the gate and follow a trail leading downhill between rolls of white sand, I think of how this bleached and shifting substrate must have challenged the pineapple barons. I learn later that doses of fertilizer sustained the pineapples, while the working mules and horses found purchase in the sand only after they were outfitted with sand shoes, metal contraptions about ten inches by eight inches, a southern variation on snow shoes.

The sandy path we travel today presents no real hardships. The plants and animals we have come to see are adapted for life in this scrub; they know how to conserve water and hide from the sun. People can learn how to do that too, but this habitat has traditionally been loved more for what it could be—pineapple plantation, golf course, housing development—than for its intrinsic worth as a unique refugium. Scrub once covered about one million acres in Florida; only about 400,000 acres remain today. Is it that we resent dunes when they're no longer attached to oceans?

An appreciation of scrub requires an extended courtship, prefer-ably during the cooler months of the year. Such effort has created a small but dedicated group of allies around the state who have fallen in love with the lichens and bromeliads, the rosemary and penny-royal, the gopher tortoises and scrub jays. Here in the Savannas, the scrub comprises about 350 acres of the 5,000 acres within its boundaries. It makes a sturdy platform for a busy railroad line. More importantly of course, it acts as a wonderful filter, cleaning the rainwater that supplies about 90 percent of the water in the Savannas. This recharge of the water table helps prevent saltwater intrusion of the aquifer, a problem that plagues many coastal communities.

The path we descend is rimmed by a profusion of palafoxia, Spanish needle, partridge pea, and sensitive briar. We pass beneath stands of sand pine and thickets of myrtle, Chapman's and sand live oaks. Lichens carpet the ground in some areas and bromeliads are thick on every branch and trunk. Our trail runs south and then loops back. The trains sound like they are bearing down on us. Between their roars, the deep hooting of a great-horned owl joins the high-pitched scold of a blue-gray gnatcatcher. Two human voices rise and fall in argument, but the wind makes it tricky to judge their distance from us. Is someone else on the trail? We try to stay focused on plant identification and the play of the fading rosy light on cumulus clouds.

Clouds greet us again the next morning as we prepare for canoeing and a short hike through the slash pine flatwoods. It has rained during the night but today's weather appears quixotic. Is sun screen or rain gear in order? Barbara scrabbles around in the back of her truck looking for her missing hat. She must settle for the only other headgear she can round up—a red plastic fireman's helmet left behind by her four-year-old. As it turns out, the gusty wind and waves of rain showers later relegate the helmet to the bottom of the canoe. Two scrub jays greet us at the canoe launch near the reserve headquarters. Near a telephone pole just inside the boundary fence, we take a quick side trip following a short path, well traveled by other pilgrims, to see the fragrant prickly apple, a tall, very endangered cactus. Its fuzzy gray arms seem to reach up in supplication.

Once on the water, we paddle for all we're worth against the elements. The warm wind pushes us around the watery heart of this reserve and we conduct a kind of haphazard transect. More than 2,000 acres of marsh, lake, and wet prairie dominate the Savannas. The water is shallow for the most part, and perfect for the wading and probing of sandhill cranes, great blue herons, and great egrets. But two natural lakes, Eden Lake and Henderson Pond, purportedly support largemouth bass, crappie, bream, and catfish in their twenty-foot depths.

A warm gust sweeps us away from a shoreline once dredged and filled to create an airstrip. The embankment is showy nonetheless, with its heads of golden aster and goldenrod dancing against a backdrop of green wax myrtle. White water lilies ride on the tannin-stained water, and red-winged blackbirds chatter noisily from clumps of pickerel weed and sagittaria. Notably absent are cattails. That's a good sign here. It means that the water is low in organic material, which is to be expected from rainwater filtering through sandy soils. It also means that for the time being, stormwater inflows are not importing excessive amounts of fertilizers or sewage from surrounding development. In shallow areas, our paddles strike a firm sandy bottom beneath the woody stems of St. John's wort. About every ten years or so, we'd be able to hike through here; large parts of the Savannas dry out completely, allowing a cyclic cleansing and renewal of plants and animals.

We curse at a young stand of melaleuca (an invasive exotic tree), but our spirits are bolstered by the sonorous call of sandhill cranes off to the south. Heading for a windbreak behind a distant tussock, we discover a patch of yellow-eyed grass in full bloom, more extensive than either of us has ever seen. The wind plays through the blades of saw grass, and all is peaceful until an immature bald eagle scatters small groups of killdeer and black ducks. Walton Road, one of two roads that bisect the Savannas, blocks our northern passage. Turning around to the south, the rain finally drives us back to our car.

The afternoon finds us on the flatwoods trail on the western side of the Savannas. Historically, stands of slash pine marched westward from here for many miles, stopping only when they met watery obstacles. Today, their ranks have been reduced to a linear fringe along the Savannas' edge. At the turn for Sandhill Crane Park and the trailhead, sandhill cranes and white ibises probe the lawns of a condominium complex. The sounds of traffic on Walton Road follow us as we start out on the flatwoods trail, and a pile of melaleuca trunks marks a battleground: park service versus exotic plant. The understory of palmetto, gallberry, and blueberry is dense and ready for a burn. A short spur trail angles off toward the marsh, where a lone sandhill crane stands in ankle-deep water. We skirt the muddy edges of large puddles where horses and wild hogs have left their mark. Trails through these flatwoods are popular with the equestrian crowd and the hogs, well, they're as difficult to remove as the melaleuca. We only walk about two miles that day, though the trail continues north for several more.

The sundews at our feet are just one indication that these woods function as a water storage area for overflows from the adjacent marshes. Florida has a love-hate relationship with water and it is played out here in the Savannas. The thirst of the burgeoning population strains supplies of freshwater from the underground aquifer; the flow of dirty storm water threatens its purity. Residents in homes built too near the water resent its intrusive and unforgiving nature. Non-native plants try to gain a foothold.

Managing the water in the Savannas to satisfy scientific and community objectives is just one of the challenges facing park managers. As with so many of Florida's smaller conservation areas, the forces that squeeze this reserve will only increase in the coming years. The east-west roads that span its interior may expand in the near future to include a new bridge, arching over the Indian River to Hutchinson Island. The controlled burns necessary to maintain the flatwoods and scrub will require both skill and diplomacy in areas so close to residential development. The fishing is good here, but the catches are high in mercury. The roar of the trains is louder than the voices of the sandhill cranes.

For the visitor, however, these issues are mere distractions, and forgivable ones at that. Big chunks of wild Florida serve one set of purposes, smaller chunks like the Savannas, quite another. The Savannas State Reserve is a small piece of wild Florida surrounded by that other Florida—tract housing and strip malls. The landscape here is readily accessible to thousands of people, many of whom desperately need a link to the Florida landscape. Perhaps a sandhill crane will engage their imaginations? Or will it be the view of a sunset from a sandy ridgetop? Whatever it is, I hope the end result is the same: the Savannas will stand as a refuge for untold numbers of plants and animals and for the human spirit as well.

The Tallahassee–St. Marks Trail

MARY TEBO

In 1984, a friend asked me to go on a hike down the old rail bed of the St. Marks Railroad. Representatives of the Florida Department of Transportation (DOT) hosted our trip. They described their dream of transforming the "abandoned transportation corridor" into a "linear recreation park." The ties, rails, and sleepers would be pulled up; the cinder bed leveled and partially paved. This would create a sixteen-mile, car-free route from Tallahassee to St. Marks for joggers, bicyclists, hikers, and horseback-riders.

I remember walking down south of u.s. 98, where the railroad became a narrow impoundment through low ground. Swamp mallow bloomed beside its banks, and cypress seemed determined to reclaim the strip of land—its knobby knees poked up between the railroad ties. "Right-of-way" seemed like a funny phrase. No matter who legally owned this long, thin swatch of property, the Florida woods would always wrestle for right of way, struggle to snatch it back with their knuckly joints and sinuous roots.

The Tallahassee–St. Marks Historic Railroad State Trail has prevailed over rebellious vegetation, however—at least for now. DOT bought the old rail line in 1984 from the Seaboard Coast Line for about $300,000. Their original intent was just to secure state ownership of the corridor for future transportation needs. But trail advocates were so convincing that, in 1986, Governor Bob Graham and his Cabinet passed a resolution to convert the right-of-way into Florida's first "rail-trail." The state legislature appropriated funds for the construction and operation of the trail the following year.

In 1989 the St. Marks Trail opened: an eight-foot-wide slab of asphalt that was 16.2 miles long, with a parallel, unpaved path for horses. The Division of Recreation and Parks of the Florida Department of Environmental Protection now manages the trail, identifying it as one of Florida's most heavily used state parks. Preservation 2000 funds later paid for a northern extension of the trail that juts north of South Capital Circle into urban Tallahassee, as well as for other abandoned rail beds around the state.

"The St. Marks Trail gets about 150,000 visits a year," said Wes Smith, park ranger. "There's a wide variety of users—young, old, bicyclists, joggers, walkers, in-line skaters, equestrians.

"It's an excellent way for people to exercise and at the same time be in the outdoors—instead of at a gym or at a track or at their house. The trail gives them some exposure to a natural setting," Smith said.

Some might be surprised that Preservation 2000 money has been used to support this park—a contrast to some of the wilderness sites these funds have preserved. But in fact, the St. Marks Trail provides an egalitarian setting for hard-core, novice, and timid outdoors enthusiasts to enjoy Florida habitats. The "All Aboard!" that used to ring out as passenger trains boarded still applies to the adapted recreation park, with a decidedly populist ring. This is an outdoor trip that all can board.

"One of the positive aspects of the trail is it brings people together," said Ken Foster, president of the St. Marks Trail Association, a community coalition. He is also the owner of About Bikes, a bicycle and skate rental center at the trailhead.

"You don't have to be a member of any particular group of people to use the trail," Foster said. "There are no economic boundaries, no racial boundaries. Recreationalists will come in from ten to twenty miles away. But we also see lots of blue collar workers riding bikes to and from work. Lots of people are just getting in a walk. Students use it to get to school. We've even seen people in wheelchairs out here.

"The trail brings people together because they're looking at each other and talking to each other," he said.

The last time I rode the trail, I went with my brother—the wild hare in my family—and my six-year-old daughter. My brother, whose bike is his main means of transportation, literally rode circles around me. My daughter traveled in a sort of rickshaw contraption, a little trailer attached to my bike. Happily passive, she beamed from the shadows of her nylon cocoon and shouted, "Go faster!" My brother, meanwhile, was blasting down the equestrian path, shearing off vines and low branches and rattling all the bolts off his aluminum-frame Gary Fisher. It was almost immediately clear to me who should be towing the rickshaw down the paved path, and we switched bikes.

We encountered several other bicyclists as we progressed, and one tricyclist—young but obviously no amateur, as he illustrated by doing a wheelie. Two skaters passed by, one clad in pads from toe to head, helmeted, and another coolly padless, dressed in cutoffs. And several people were out walking.

We passed Woodville Pentacostal Holiness Church, with its portasign that proclaimed, "We love our pastors!" There were parking spaces marked for the "pastor" and "pastorette." We passed Ace High Stables and the remains of an old sawmill. We passed a trailer park named "Buddyville," old roads named Main and Lee and new roads named Summerwind and Hidden Valley.

But we also saw goldenrod and dog fennel blooming in the copper glow of the clear fall afternoon. The silvery leaves of narrow-leaved aster clung to the sandy shoulders of the trail, and the occasional beautyberry bushes were bright with purple fruit. Scrub oaks grew thick along stretches of the trail, gluttonous for the sunlight that fell along this open corridor. Winged sumac was just beginning to flame red. South of Woodville, we drank in the open, spare vista of several acres of longleaf flatwoods. And south of that, we began to see cabbage palms among the trees, giving our surroundings the unmistakable look of Gulf coastal hammock.

That old St. Marks Railroad must have been a puny tunnel through a tangle of vegetation. The first railroad built in Florida, it carried passengers back and forth through this same space from 1837 to 1959. Mules pulled the cars until steam locomotives took over in 1856. Stories of the mule-drawn train tell of rails so warped they curved up into the air. Someone was sent ahead to hold down the end of each rail until the cars came to it, and then this human railroad stake would run ahead to weigh down the next rail. Fires burning through the piney woods practically licked the sides of the railway cars but, as one traveler relates in *The Story of Florida Railroads:* "On we hurried like salamanders."

For most of the 1800s, St. Marks was Tallahassee's gateway to the world. Overland travel was arduous; boats were the preferred means of transportation. Even today, it is not hard to imagine that old passageway hacked out of the woods, running beneath huge pines, oaks, and magnolias, disappearing intermittently into brown swamp water studded with cypress knees.

"You might see a turkey, possums, raccoons, snakes," says Ken

Foster, when I ask him what wildlife people have spotted from the trail. Sightings are usually on the southern, more isolated portion of the trail, he said. "Actually, we've even seen fish on the trail. There's been huge flooding—the trail was under two feet of water in places and we saw fish swimming on the trail."

Riding the trail today, people are still using it to go. Somewhere. Are they going away, or toward? Are they transporting themselves spiritually, or are they just going to work?

Considering these questions, I became newly aware of the north Florida woods pressed close against us, the mosquitoes, the crickets, the sun, the seeming silence, the rustling trees, the birds calling.

Protected not just from the hazard but the din of motor traffic, I could hear the wilderness of Florida. It is a voice with leaves and wings and roots and claws. Forever usurping right-of-way, wilderness still breathes heavy on travelers of the St. Marks Trail, says, "I am here. You may not ignore me." Thousands of people hear it, consciously or unconsciously. It sings and sighs and shouts.

South of U.S. Highway 98, I bounced over the landmark I'd been looking for—a bumpy cypress knee, growing up through asphalt.

Contributors

BILL BELLEVILLE specializes in writing about the natural world, traveling from his home in Sanford throughout Florida, as well as to Latin America, Australia, and the Arctic Circle. His credits include over 1,500 articles with bylines in *Sierra, Islands, Audubon, Newsweek, Reader's Digest,* and *American Way,* and real-time overseas field reports for the Discovery Channel's website. He recently wrote and co-produced a Florida Public Television special on William Bartram's trip up the St. Johns River and has completed a book—*The St. Johns: The Unseen River.* He has won a number of awards, including the Florida Wildlife Federation's Environmental Writer of the Year, and most recently, Florida Audubon's Hal Scott Memorial Award for "his work as a nature writer and film maker."

AL BURT worked for the *Miami Herald* for more than forty years and was a roving Florida columnist for twenty years. He has written four books: *Al Burt's Florida: Snowbirds, Sand Castles, and Self-rising Crackers; Papa Doc; Florida: A Place in the Sun;* and *Becalmed in the Mullet Latitudes.*

ARCHIE CARR (1909–1987) was an eminent naturalist, writer, conservationist, and world authority on sea turtles. He was graduate research professor of zoology at the University of Florida, Gainesville. During his illustrious career he won numerous awards and honors, including the Daniel Giraud Elliot Medal of the National Academy of Sciences, the O. Henry Award for short-story writing, the Hal Borland Award of the National Audubon Society, and the designation of Eminent Ecologist by the Ecological Society of America. Throughout his life he wrote on many aspects of natural history, but he was particularly entranced by the wildlife and ecosystems of Florida, where he lived for more than fifty years. Among his many books are *Ulendo: Travels of a Naturalist In and Out of Africa, So Excellent a Fishe, The Windward Road,* and *A Naturalist in Florida: A Celebration of Eden.*

SUSAN CERULEAN has worked on conservation issues in Florida for the past fifteen years and presently coordinates the Florida Game and Fresh Water Fish Commission's Watchable Wildlife program. Among her publications are *Planting a Refuge for Wildlife* and the *Florida Wildlife Viewing Guide,* coauthored with Ann Morrow. She writes a monthly environmental column for the *Tallahassee Democrat* and is at work on her second book, *Looking after God's Birds,* which concerns the conservation of swallow-tailed kites. In 1997, Cerulean was named Environmental Educator of the Year by the Governor's Council for Sustainable Florida.

DEBBIE DRAKE is currently the assistant secretary for conservation programs at the California Resources Agency. While at The Nature Conservancy in Florida, Debbie was a leading advocate for land and water conservation. Her efforts helped secure more than $1.8 billion in public funding to acquire and manage the state's conservation lands.

LOLA HASKINS has published six books of poetry, most recently *Extranjera.* Her fifth collection, *Hunger,* won the Iowa Poetry Prize in 1992. A further collection, *Desire Lines: New and Selected Poems,* is forthcoming. Her work has appeared widely in periodicals, such as *Christian Science Monitor, Georgia Review, Sojourner, Southern Review,* and *Prairie*

Schooner. She teaches computer science at the University of Florida and lives on a farm outside Gainesville.

JULIE HAUSERMAN has been writing about Florida's environment since 1986 and has won numerous awards for her work. A former environmental columnist for the *Tallahassee Democrat,* Hauserman now works as a Capital bureau reporter for the *St. Petersburg Times.*

CARL HIAASEN is a columnist with the *Miami Herald* and author of several novels, including *Lucky You, Tourist Season, Stormy Weather, Skintight, Double Whammy,* and *Striptease.*

JOE HUTTO is a wildlife artist and the author of the critically acclaimed *Illumination in the Flatwoods: A Season with the Wild Turkey.*

JEFF KLINKENBERG is a columnist for the *St. Petersburg Times* and the author of two collections of essays about the state: *Real Florida: Key Lime Pies, Worm Fiddlers, a Man Called Frog, and Other Endangered Species* and *Dispatches from the Land of Flowers.*

ANN MORROW is a biologist and freelance writer who has been writing about the Florida environment for the past thirteen years. She coauthored the *Florida Wildlife Viewing Guide* and *Florida Trails: A Guide to Florida's Natural Habitats* with Susan Cerulean. Ann writes two monthly columns for the *Tallahassee Democrat*—one on environmental issues and another on children and nature.

JANISSE RAY, a poet and essayist, has published in numerous magazines and literary journals, including *Hope, Orion, Talking River Review,* and *Snake Nation Review.* For two years she was associate editor of *Florida Wildlife Magazine.* She won the 1996 Writer's Conferences and Festivals Nonfiction Award, and the 1996 Merriam Frontier Award, which included publication of a chapbook of poetry (about biology and place), *Naming the Unseen.* Her *Ecology of a Cracker Childhood* is forthcoming.

JEFF RIPPLE, a natural history writer and photographer, has authored five books of interpretive natural history, including *Florida: The Natural*

Wonders, Sea Turtles, The Florida Keys, and *Southwest Florida's Wetland Wilderness.* He was awarded the Outstanding Journalist Award for 1997 by the Florida Audubon Society for his collective works. Ripple has completed a book about manatees and dugongs, forthcoming in 1999, and is working on a collection of essays about southern swamps and estuaries. He lives with his wife, Renée, and their three cats in a small house in the woods near Gainesville, Florida.

RENÉE RIPPLE, a poet and freelance editor, is coordinator of stewardship and donations for the University of Florida Foundation.

PATRICK D. SMITH is a native of Mississippi. He is the author of six novels: *The River Is Home, The Beginning, Forever Island, Angel City, Allapattah,* and *A Land Remembered.* His nonfiction book, *In Search of the Russian Bear,* was written after a tour of the former Soviet Union as a guest of the Soviet Writer's Union. He has been nominated three times for the Pulitzer Prize and was nominated for the 1985 Nobel Prize for Literature for his lifetime work as a writer. Smith lives with his wife, Iris, on Merritt Island.

DON STAP, the author of *A Parrot without a Name,* has written articles for such magazines as *Audubon, Smithsonian, Orion, Sierra,* and *International Wildlife.* He teaches at the University of Central Florida.

MARY TEBO is a native Floridian, born on the banks of the St. Johns River, and a twenty-six-year resident of Tallahassee. She has worked with *Florida Wildlife* magazine and Tall Timbers Research Station and has studied and practiced both biology and creative writing. She enjoys pointing out the everyday connections between people and the natural world. She now lives and works in Knoxville, Tennessee.

RANDY WAYNE WHITE is the author of five novels (*Sanibel Flats, The Heat Islands, The Man Who Invented Florida, Captiva,* and *North of Havana*) and one collection of essays (*Batfishing in the Rainforest*). As a monthly columnist for *Outside,* his travels have taken him around the world.